Help Yourself to Live Longer

This book is dedicated to my parents Joan and Dennis, and also to Edna – may you all enjoy becoming supercentenarians. Also in memory of Alex, who didn't quite make it that far.

Teach Yourself®

Help Yourself to Live Longer

Paul Jenner

For UK order enquiries: please contact Bookpoint Ltd,
130 Milton Park, Abingdon, Oxon OX14 4SB.
Telephone: +44 (0) 1235 827720. Fax: +44 (0) 1235 400454.
Lines are open 09.00–17.00, Monday to Saturday, with a 24-hour
message answering service. Details about our titles and how to
order are available at www.teachyourself.com

For USA order enquiries: please contact McGraw-Hill Customer
Services, PO Box 545, Blacklick, OH 43004-0545, USA.
Telephone: 1-800-722-4726. Fax: 1-614-755-5645.

For Canada order enquiries: please contact McGraw-Hill
Ryerson Ltd, 300 Water St, Whitby, Ontario L1N 9B6, Canada.
Telephone: 905 430 5000. Fax: 905 430 5020.

Long renowned as the authoritative source for self-guided
learning – with more than 50 million copies sold worldwide –
the **Teach Yourself** series includes over 500 titles in the fields
of languages, crafts, hobbies, business, computing and education.

British Library Cataloguing in Publication Data: a catalogue record
for this title is available from the British Library.

Library of Congress Catalog Card Number: on file.

First published in UK 2008 by Hodder Education, part of
Hachette UK, 338 Euston Road, London NW1 3BH.

This edition published 2010.

Previously published as *Teach Yourself Living Longer, Living Well*.

The **Teach Yourself** name is a registered trade mark of
Hodder Headline.

Copyright © 2008, 2010 Paul Jenner

Typeset by MPS Limited, a Macmillan Company.

Printed in Great Britain for Hodder Education, an Hachette UK
Company, 338 Euston Road, London NW1 3BH, by CPI Cox &
Wyman, Reading, Berkshire RG1 8EX.

The publisher has used its best endeavours to ensure that the URLs
for external websites referred to in this book are correct and active
at the time of going to press. However, the publisher and the
author have no responsibility for the websites and can make no
guarantee that a site will remain live or that the content will remain
relevant, decent or appropriate.

Hachette UK's policy is to use papers that are natural, renewable
and recyclable products and made from wood grown in sustainable
forests. The logging and manufacturing processes are expected to
conform to the environmental regulations of the country of origin.

Impression number   10 9 8 7 6 5 4 3 2 1
Year   2014 2013 2012 2011 2010

Acknowledgements

A very special thank you to Victoria Roddam, my publisher at Hodder Education.

Image credits

Front cover: © Oleksiy Maksymenko/Alamy

Back cover: © Jakub Semeniuk/iStockphoto.com, © Royalty-Free/Corbis, © agencyby/iStockphoto.com, © Andy Cook/iStockphoto.com, © Christopher Ewing/iStockphoto.com, © zebicho – Fotolia.com, © Geoffrey Holman/iStockphoto.com, © Photodisc/Getty Images, © James C. Pruitt/iStockphoto.com, © Mohamed Saber – Fotolia.com

Contents

Meet the author

You know you're getting older when you ring friends and are increasingly told, 'Oh, he's out running'. Or, 'She's at her yoga class'. Or, 'They're at a Buddhist retreat'.

It happens to the majority of people eventually. If it happens when you're a teenager you're really lucky. But that's rare. Mostly it happens fairly naturally between 40 and 50. After that it takes a crisis. But a crisis always comes. In my case I was pretty fortunate. I was only 35. Hardly a teenager but still young enough for concern about my health and how long I might live to make a huge difference.

Since then I've downsized to Spain, completely changed the way I eat (masses of antioxidants), fallen in love, improved my sex life (I wrote *Teach Yourself: Have Great Sex* as well as *Teach Yourself: Get Intimate with Tantric Sex*), become a regular exerciser, become more spiritual, learned to relax and become extremely happy (I also wrote *Teach Yourself: How to Be Happier*). None of those things guarantee me a long life but all of them improve my chances.

In these pages I hope you'll find plenty of things you can incorporate into your lifestyle and improve your chances, as I have done.

They say only two things are certain in life. But there is a third. One lifetime is really not enough.

Paul Jenner, Spain, 2010

Only got a minute?

▶ Many illnesses, including dementia and about a third of cancers, are thought to be associated with incorrect diet – eat plenty of foods high in antioxidants, use monounsaturated fats and omega-3 polyunsaturated fats in place of other fats, and take supplements if necessary.

▶ The more you exercise, within reason, the greater your chance of living longer – and you'll be happier, too.

▶ Happiness is itself important to health and longevity. It doesn't fall out of the sky but you can actually *choose* to be happy and you can learn to banish negative thinking by using cognitive therapy.

▶ When you're not exercising, learn to be relaxed physically.

- ▶ And relax mentally, too. Stress (unless it's the pleasurable sort called 'eustress') is bad for you. Try meditation or cognitive therapy.

- ▶ Make sure your life isn't shortened unnecessarily. Live prudently: keep your exposure to carcinogens (cancer-causing substances) to a minimum; especially don't smoke; drink alcohol only very moderately; avoid drugs; never get sunburn; drive carefully; wear a helmet when sensible; practise safe sex; have appropriate medical checks and don't put off going to the doctor if you suspect something serious.

- ▶ Love generates chemicals that not only make you feel good but actually are good for your health.

- ▶ Frequent sex is associated not only with a more youthful appearance but also with a longer life.

- ▶ People who attend religious services every week gain, on average, two to three years compared with those who don't – just being spiritual helps a little, too.

1

Why we age

In this chapter you will learn:
- *that not everything ages*
- *the role played by your genes*
- *the role played by your lifestyle.*

I'd like to introduce you to a couple of rather interesting families. First, the Blanding family. Mrs Blanding is now in her fifties and pregnant. She's been pregnant a lot of her adult life. But even more incredible is that, apart from having put on some weight, Mrs Blanding hardly looks a day older than she did at 20. And it's not just a question of appearance. On most physiological measurements Mrs Blanding has barely aged at all in the past 30 years. Her sisters and brothers are just as fortunate.

The Sebastes are equally extraordinary, but in a rather different way. Some members of the family have aged rapidly, dying before reaching their teenage years. Others have done better but were nevertheless old before they were 50. One member of the family – affectionately known as Red – has reached 106. But the record age goes to a relative up in the Aleutian Islands who made it to... 205!

Yes, as you probably guessed, the Sebastes is not a human family but a family of fish – rockfish – ranging from *Sebastes dalli*, the shortest lived, through our friend Red (the redbanded rockfish, *Sebastes babcocki*) right up to *Sebastes aleutianus*, living specimens of which were born when Napoleon was retreating from Moscow.

And the Blandings? Justin Congdon knows them about as well as anybody. He used to be a trapper but later directed his skills at more positive goals, studying turtles at the University of Michigan's E. S. George Reserve – *Blanding's* turtles. His observations showed that they (and possibly other turtle species) barely senesce, that's to say, deteriorate physically, with the passing years. Death comes from being hit by a car or mauled by a raccoon. And when it is caused by infectious diseases, it is no more common in older turtles than younger ones.

The incredible fact is that there are animals that get older *without ageing*. And, at last, scientists are beginning to unlock their secrets.

The gene theory of ageing

Clearly, the fact that the many changes associated with old age in human beings appear more or less together suggests some central mechanism, rather than a whole series of different mechanisms. You don't, for example, ever find a 90-year-old with all the normal signs of ageing except for having the beautiful elastic skin of a child, or the long, glowing hair of a teenager. At the end of the line there has to be one thing that controls everything.

Many scientists believe the 'central mechanism' is in the genes. We know that drastically accelerated ageing in humans (for example, in Werner's, Cockayne and Hutchinson-Gilford syndromes) has to do with certain genetic mutations. And through gene manipulation scientists have already extended the lifespan of mice by up to 50 per cent. So that seems pretty compelling.

But how would genetic variation for lifespan come about naturally within a species? The answer is in the same way that everything else comes about, by evolution through natural selection. Some people therefore call it the *evolutionary theory* of ageing. Genes that cause death before sexual maturity get deselected, because the organism wouldn't have any offspring to pass them on to. But now consider genes that are beneficial in youth but dangerous in old age. Those genes *would* be selected, because the organism would reproduce successfully and pass them on before succumbing later to the negative effects of the genes. This is the way that death becomes genetically programmed.

In one experiment, only older fruit flies (*Drosophila*) were allowed to reproduce, with the result that the succeeding generations of flies aged more slowly and lived longer (because evolution was thereby *forced* to select genes for that). If a law were to be passed that no human beings could reproduce under the age of 40 then human beings would live longer on average than they do now. After a while the age limit could be raised to 50 and then 60. Almost certainly it would become normal to live well beyond 100 because, by this method, genes for longevity would be selected and genes that shortened life would be deselected.

But where does all this get you right now? You're stuck with the genes you've got. Right?

Not exactly. I can tell you two things you can try so as to manipulate your 'central genetic mechanism'.

You see, you may have genes that aren't 'switched on'. Genes that could extend your life. Genes such as SIRT-1 (also known as Sirtuin-1). It would seem that in times of famine this gene would have kept our ancestors alive on a starvation diet. That's why it's known as the 'survival gene'. And you can activate yours, it seems, by reproducing those same conditions. Calorie restriction (CR) works spectacularly well in mice, it works on rhesus monkeys, and the evidence so far is that it has the same physiological effects on humans. I'll be telling you all about it in the next chapter, but you probably won't want to do it because CR is very tough indeed.

Is there an easier way of turning on that gene? Possibly. When vines are attacked by certain bacteria or fungi they respond by producing a substance known as resveratrol. In other words, it's the vine's response to a certain kind of stress. Transfer that substance into a completely different kind of organism, say a mouse or a human being and, miraculously, it still seems to have the ability to communicate with that new organism. It seems to make the new organism believe that it's facing a stress that requires SIRT-1 to be activated. Scientists are still working on it, but whatever the mechanism turns out to be, mice fed resveratrol live longer. Human trials have so far been limited but the evidence is that the effect should be the same.

Another theory of ageing at the intracellular level has to do with telomeres. Inside your cells your genes are strung out like threads called chromosomes, and the telomeres are the 'caps' at the ends of the chromosomes. Each time your DNA (that stands for deoxyribonucleic acid, the chemical from which your genes are made) replicates, the telomeres tend to get shorter. The theory is that when the telomeres get below a certain length the cells themselves can no longer divide and either malfunction or die. In fact, Leonard Hayflick (b. 1928) a Professor of Anatomy at the University of California, proved in a test tube that human cells can, indeed, divide only a limited number of times, which came as a surprise to many. This is known as the Hayflick limit. Normal animal and human cells are, in this sense, 'mortal', whereas cancer cells are 'immortal'.

If telomeres are the key, then they may provide another explanation for the apparently beneficial effects of resveratrol, because it seems that resveratrol has a protective effect on them. So taking resveratrol, in one form or another, seems like a reasonable strategy. However, among primates, humans have the shortest telomeres but the longest lifespans. And mice have long telomeres and short lifespans. What's more, the human body produces something called telomerase that actually has the ability to elongate telomeres, so the effects of division are not quite so clear-cut after all. For the moment, then, the theory of telomeres and ageing is speculative.

These things apart, your maximum potential age is for the moment down to 'luck'. The luck, that is, of the genes that fate has dealt you. Some people just *do* get a better start in life than others and if you're reading this book it's already too late to change certain things. If you're a woman, congratulations! Depending on where you live, you're already likely to survive something like four to eight years longer than if you'd been born a boy. Smart choice.

You're also lucky if in your family tree there are relatives who lived into their eighties and nineties, because there's a good chance that you'll do at least as well, and probably better. Confirmation of this comes from researchers at Boston University in the USA who studied the 'genetic signatures' of 1,055 centenarians. They identified 33 single nucleotide polymorphisms (SNPs) – essentially variants in DNA that other people don't have. Known affectionately to biochemists as 'Snips', these are basically DNA copying errors that have had the fortuitous effect of extending life. It's predicted that about 150 will eventually be found.

So does that mean there's no point in trying to follow a healthier lifestyle? That the day of your death has already been decided? That fatalism rules? Not at all. The proof is in the huge leap in life expectancy in the last century. That's far too short a time for genes to have been involved. It *must* have been to do with lifestyle, nutrition, hygiene and healthcare. Who knows how much further we can go with those things?

Who knows what anybody's potential is in genetic terms, anyway? Maybe few of us come near it. So the practical way of living longer is to get as close to your potential as possible. To avoid harm. To protect yourself.

When Linus Pauling, the great champion of vitamin C, was born back in 1901, life expectancy for an American male was just 48 years. For an American male born today it's a few months over 75 (and for a female, almost 81). Pauling himself beat life expectancy handsomely and died at the age of 93. Was he just 'lucky'? Or could it have had something to do with protecting himself from free radicals?

The free radical theory of ageing

The free radical theory of ageing was developed by Denham Harman in the 1950s. Free radicals are found in certain foods. Essentially they're atoms that lack electrons and, to remedy that, they may steal them from your DNA. The DNA damage may in turn lead to malfunction and cancer. Free radicals have also been linked to Alzheimer's disease, arteriosclerosis, deafness, melanin abnormalities, arthritis and diabetes.

Vitamins and some other nutrients are antioxidants. That's to say, they have a spare electron they can 'give' to the free radicals, thus neutralizing them. Those antioxidants come mostly in fruits and vegetables, which are therefore an essential part of any recipe for living longer. It's not possible to say that taking an abnormally high level of antioxidants lengthens anybody's maximum potential lifespan, but it is possible to say that eating insufficient antioxidants shortens actual lifespan. And many people do eat insufficient. If you're in that category, taking supplements, as Linus Pauling recommended, makes sense.

The same thinking applies to many areas of your life. If you're not taking much exercise, if you're stressed and unhappy, if you're not making time for friends, family and your love life, if you're not taking care to avoid accidents and dangerous habits of all kinds, and if you haven't yet discovered any spiritual feelings, then, yes, this book can teach you how to live longer than you would have done. Ten extra years is easily possible. Even 20. Even more.

Don't believe me? Then reflect on this. If you smoke, then by giving up you stand a 50:50 chance of extending your life by 21 years. If one thing can make such a massive difference, think what two or three could do. Or four or five?

How are you doing so far?
Here's a little quiz. Don't let it worry you. It isn't going to make any gloomy predictions. On the contrary, it's going to help you identify the areas of your lifestyle that could do with some attention.

And once you've done that, you've taken your first step to living those extra years. And living them well.

Make a note of the statements you most closely agree with.

1   a   *I eat several fruits every day.*
     b   *I eat at least one fruit every day.*
     c   *I seldom eat fruit.*

2   a   *I always have two or three different vegetables with lunch and dinner.*
     b   *I have at least one type of vegetable each day.*
     c   *I don't like vegetables very much.*

3   a   *I eat little or no animal fat.*
     b   *I eat animal fat in moderation.*
     c   *I eat lots of animal fat.*

4   a   *I never add sugar to food or drink and eat hardly any sugary food.*
     b   *I have sugar in moderation.*
     c   *I love sugar.*

5   a   *I never eat processed foods or junk food.*
     b   *I use processed foods moderately and eat junk food occasionally.*
     c   *I'm so busy that I have to rely on convenience foods most of the time.*

6   a   *I'm well below average weight for my height and build.*
     b   *I'm about average weight.*
     c   *I'm overweight.*

7   a   *I take vitamin and mineral supplements regularly.*
     b   *I take vitamin supplements when I'm feeling a bit low.*
     c   *I never take vitamin or mineral supplements.*

8   a   *I take vigorous exercise at least five days a week.*
     b   *I get a bit of exercise most weekends.*
     c   *I never exercise.*

9   a *I like to take on lots of new and different kinds of mental challenges.*
     b *I keep mentally stimulated with things I know I like.*
     c *I haven't learned anything new recently and I keep away from situations that are mentally challenging.*

10 a *I'm not at all stressed.*
     b *There are things that stress me every day but I can handle them.*
     c *I feel stressed most of the time.*

11 a *I seldom get angry.*
     b *I get angry when it's deserved.*
     c *I feel angry a lot.*

12 a *I sleep seven hours a night.*
     b *I sleep five to six hours a night.*
     c *I sleep nine to ten hours a night.*

13 a *I feel happy most of the time.*
     b *I feel happy quite often.*
     c *I feel unhappy most of the time.*

14 a *I've never smoked.*
     b *I used to smoke but I've given up.*
     c *I smoke.*

15 a *I drink alcohol occasionally with a meal.*
     b *I drink alcohol most days but only in moderation.*
     c *Alcohol is a feature of my life.*

16 a *I sunbathe very cautiously and I never get burnt.*
     b *I like to sunbathe when the opportunity arises and, just occasionally, I do get a bit burnt.*
     c *My idea of a holiday is sunbathing all day and I always end up like a lobster.*

17　a　*I have health check-ups when there's a reason.*
　　b　*I'm one of the 'worried well' and have every health check going.*
　　c　*I keep well away from doctors.*

18　a　*I'm in a committed and supportive relationship; I love and feel loved.*
　　b　*I was in a very happy relationship and have wonderful memories to cherish.*
　　c　*I don't believe in love.*

19　a　*I have a wide circle of friends and relatives whom I see often.*
　　b　*My partner is the focus of my life but I do see friends and relatives now and then.*
　　c　*I hardly ever socialize.*

20　a　*The physical side of our relationship is as important as ever.*
　　b　*Sex has become an occasional thing.*
　　c　*I don't have sex very often and I don't like it.*

21　a　*I'm a very spiritual person.*
　　b　*I don't have strong spiritual feelings but I'm perfectly happy with that.*
　　c　*Life is futile.*

22　a　*I face the future with optimism because I know my life has a point and, whatever happens, there will be some kind of afterlife.*
　　b　*I enjoy my life and I'm not worried about death.*
　　c　*I'm very worried about dying.*

How did you get on?

Score three for every (a), two for every (b) and one for every (c).

60 or more. If you carry on like this you're very likely to live to a great age but you'll probably still find some new ideas in this book.

50–60. You live in a very healthy way and you'll obviously be receptive to any new ideas you can get from these pages, which is very important.

40–50. You have a moderately healthy lifestyle and nothing particularly to worry about but with a little effort you could improve your well-being considerably.

30–40. You're probably rather resistant to what you see as cranky health advice but, as you'll discover when you read on, it really isn't cranky at all.

Under 30. You've really not been looking after yourself but you wouldn't be reading this if you weren't willing to make some necessary changes. So that's a good start.

Making the most of this book

The idea of the test is really only to give you some hints about what's good for your well-being and longevity and what isn't. But, of course, it can only be very general. So don't take the results too seriously.

The important thing is to be open to any ideas that are new to you and then to implement them gradually. Take your time. There's no rush. Some of the things may appeal to you straight away while others may seem daunting. But if you can just make a start on those that are least appealing to you, they'll probably come to seem more normal in a little while.

Give yourself, maybe, a year to implement everything. The mind and body need time to adjust to new ideas and new routines. But that doesn't mean you can put off taking the first steps. Begin today. Good luck!

10 THINGS TO REMEMBER

1 *Some animals barely age.*

2 *Ageing is probably controlled by genes.*

3 *Genetically manipulated mice have lived 50 per cent longer than normal.*

4 *It's possible that in human beings there are inactive survival genes capable of extending life.*

5 *Scientists so far know two possible ways of 'turning on' survival genes.*

6 *Ageing may also be connected to the length of telomeres – the 'caps' at the end of chromosomes.*

7 *Another theory of ageing is that it's caused by free radical damage to DNA.*

8 *Free radical damage can be reduced by a diet high in antioxidants.*

9 *For the time being the best strategy for living longer is to tackle a whole range of issues – keep an open mind.*

10 *It can take the body a long time to adjust to changes in food, exercise and other aspects of lifestyle, so give yourself a year or two to implement everything in this book.*

2

Food

In this chapter you will learn:
- *how antioxidants in fruits and vegetables fight cancer*
- *how eating the right fat will protect your arteries*
- *which 'wonderfoods' might help you live longer*
- *why restricting your calorie intake could extend your life.*

It was going to be a busy day and, as usual, Marie-Louise Meilleur began it with a breakfast of two bowls of oatmeal. It was her birthday, Friday 29 August 1997, and quite a lot of family were expected. She didn't know exactly how many but usually around 40 turned up. It could easily be more when you have over 200 living descendants, including great-great-great grandchildren. And, on top of that, there were all the politicians who were coming. Because this was a rather special birthday. The birthday of the world's proven oldest person. Her 117th.

It might seem a little strange to mention what Mrs Meilleur ate for breakfast. But oats have rather special qualities. They contain a particular kind of gummy fibre called beta glucans which makes them very effective at lowering the harmful type of cholesterol known as low-density lipoprotein (LDL) and raising the beneficial sort known as high-density lipoprotein (HDL). In plain language, they stop your arteries from getting clogged up.

That's not all that oats can do. They also contain protease inhibitors that combat certain viruses and carcinogens in the digestive tract. They help regulate blood sugar and insulin levels. They're anti-inflammatory. And they protect against diverticulitis and haemorrhoids. Mrs Meilleur's diet was unusual in another way. For many, many years – no one is sure exactly how many – she ate mostly plant foods. Some of them, as we'll see in a moment, contain extremely powerful anti-ageing chemicals.

The fact that Mrs Meilleur ate plenty of oats, vegetables and fruits doesn't, of course, *prove* that her diet was in any way connected with her membership of one of the world's most exclusive clubs – the supercentenarians (those over 110), who presently number something like 450 in the entire world.

But what we do know is that *on average,* health-conscious people who pay attention to their diet live longer than those who don't. A 21-year study by the German Cancer Research Centre found that both health-conscious vegetarians and *moderate* meat eaters who ate vegetables, fruits, whole grains, nuts and seeds in abundance lived significantly longer than the general population.

Insight

Many illnesses, including about a third of cancers, are thought to be associated with incorrect diet. Given what we now know about the nutrients in food, that's hardly surprising. Plants are absolutely packed with all kinds of anti-ageing substances, many of them more powerful than our best drugs.

There's a logic behind it. Human beings, after all, evolved on a 'Stone Age' diet based mainly on plants – fruits, vegetables, nuts and seeds – along with a small quantity of fish and *lean* meat (containing about five times less fat than today's average domestic animal). Going even further back, our ancestors would have consumed vastly more of certain nutrients than we do. A 7-kg (15-lb) monkey, for example, takes in around 600 mg of vitamin C per day. Broadly speaking, pound for pound, that's 100 times more vitamin C than most of us get nowadays.

Of course, monkeys aren't people. But quite a few scientists have concluded that the level of vitamins, minerals and other significant nutrients in the typical Western diet is far too low. What's more, even when we do eat the same kinds of foods as our Stone Age forebears we still end up with fewer nutrients, firstly because the soil is often depleted, secondly because the food is less fresh, and most of all because modern processing strips the vital substances away. Milling wheat, for example, *removes*:

▶ *86 per cent of vitamin E*
▶ *81 per cent of vitamin B3*
▶ *80 per cent of vitamin B2*
▶ *77 per cent of vitamin B1*
▶ *72 per cent of vitamin B6*
▶ *67 per cent of the folic acid.*

The general principle of healthy eating, then, is this: *you can only eat so much in a day, so make sure it's nutritious.*

In other words, avoid 'empty calories', that is, foods that contain very few vitamins and minerals (sweets, crisps, 'junk food'). In order to make sure you're getting enough of the nutrients for health and happiness, your diet each day should include:

▶ *whole grains, such as rice, barley and wholemeal bread, as the foundation of at least one meal*
▶ *vegetables, including green leafy vegetables (about four cups)*
▶ *fruit (about four cups)*
▶ *nuts, seeds and legumes (about one cup).*

Insight

When food is lacking important nutrient minerals (for example, calcium, magnesium, zinc, manganese, chromium, selenium and many others), toxic metals (such as mercury, lead, aluminium and cadmium) get into the body's enzyme binding sites instead. That causes the alteration of possibly thousands of vital enzymes with serious health implications. That's why I insist on whole foods, which are high in the necessary macrominerals and trace minerals.

How some foods fight ageing

Is it really true that certain plant foods can, to some extent, protect us from the effects of getting older? Yes, it is. In fact, the science is well established. Our cells contain strands of deoxyribonucleic acid (DNA) which is where our genes (the blueprints for our bodies) are held. The DNA comes under attack thousands of times a day by substances known as free radicals (sometimes referred to as reactive oxygen species – ROS), which can be found in certain foods. A free radical is an atom that lacks an electron. And it doesn't care where it gets it from. Free radicals could steal them from your DNA. They could steal them from your proteins. And they could steal them from the fat in your body, setting off a devastating chain reaction causing a whole succession of cells to crumble.

Most of the time free radical damage to the DNA is instantly repaired but now and then something gets missed. And when that happens and the cell reproduces, the error – the damage – also gets reproduced. Over the years the errors mount up. Billions of cells no longer conform to the original blueprint. The mutations are irreversible. We are old. We may have cancer.

But there's good news. There is a way of combating free radicals and that's to send in antioxidants. In fact, you'd die very quickly if it weren't for antioxidants. They have a sort of 'spare' electron that they can give to a free radical and thus neutralize it. Antioxidants can be made in the body but, like free radicals, they're also found in certain foods. So one of the secrets of living longer is pretty obvious. Eat fewer free radicals and more antioxidants. Antioxidants are abundant in a lot of plant foods. Free radicals are abundant in fat.

The problem with fat is that it becomes rancid very quickly. That's to say, it combines with oxygen or, in the jargon, it becomes peroxidized. When that happens, the dreaded free radicals are created. The higher the temperature, the quicker it occurs.

Insight

If you want to get an idea of what becoming peroxidized actually means, lay a piece of fat meat out in the sun for a few minutes. *That's* what can happen to your body. Which is why you should always store oils in a cool, dark place and use olive oil for cooking – it has a far lower tendency to create dangerous free radicals when heated.

HOW TO MINIMIZE THE INTAKE OF FREE RADICALS

1 *Cut down on all fats – they shouldn't form more than 30 per cent of your total calorie intake (the typical Western diet is 40 per cent fat).*
2 *When you consume fat, use the healthiest kinds. Reduce:*
   ▷ *trans-fatty acids – these are found in lamb, beef, dairy products and margarine (which means cakes and biscuits as well)*
   ▷ *hydrogenated or partially hydrogenated oils (which are, in fact, trans-fatty acids)*
   ▷ *solidified oils (they've been hydrogenated)*
   ▷ *saturated fats – which are mostly found in animal products*
   ▷ *Omega-6 polyunsaturated fatty acids (PUFAs) – found in animal products and vegetable oils.*
3 *Use instead:*
   ▷ *Monounsaturated fats – olive oil (see below)*
   ▷ *Omega-3 polyunsaturated fatty acids (PUFAs) – found in oily fish, rapeseed (canola), soy, walnut and flaxseed oils (see below).*

Insight

Not so long ago polyunsaturated vegetable fats were thought to be far better for you than animal fats. In fact, you may well have heeded the advice and switched. And, indeed, it's essential to eat a certain amount because polyunsaturated fats are vital and can't be made in the body. But we now know that too high a level of Omega-6 polyunsaturated fats (the commonest) is just as dangerous in its way as cholesterol – see the entry on Omega-3 fatty acids later in this chapter (see page 26).

Raw food versus cooked food

Which is most nutritious, raw food or cooked food? You'd probably answer raw food. But it's just not that simple.

In favour of raw food:

▶ *Vitamin degradation due to cooking, after adjusting for water loss, is in the range of 10–25 per cent. The vitamins most affected are vitamin C and folic acid (folate).*
▶ *Generally, raw food is lower on the Glycaemic Index than cooked food – that's to say it releases energy slowly and doesn't cause a sudden (and harmful) jump in blood sugar.*
▶ *Boiling can leach nutrients away.*
▶ *Cooking reduces or destroys some protease inhibitors – substances that fight cancer and combat viruses.*

In favour of cooked food:

▶ *The bioavailability of many vitamins may actually increase with cooking. In other words, there may be fewer vitamins in the cooked food but your body nevertheless ends up absorbing more.*
▶ *Cooked starch is two to 12 times more digestible than uncooked starch.*
▶ *Minerals in food are by and large unaffected by heat.*
▶ *Cooking destroys certain substances ('antinutrients') that prevent many nutrients being digested.*

(Contd)

Of course, it all depends on the actual food but, in general, the best approach seems to be a compromise. Cook appropriate food a little but not too much. Take beta-carotene, for example, an important vitamin that's abundant in carrots. According to some researchers, only around 2 per cent of all that wonderful beta-carotene can actually be absorbed by the body if the carrot is raw. Lightly cooking the carrot, however, significantly increases the amount of the vitamin that can be taken in by two to five times. But here's the catch. Apply more heat and quite a lot of the beta-carotene gets converted into substances known as 13- or 9-cis isomers. They're just not usable by the body.

Or consider meat and fish. Pretty unappetizing and, in some cases, downright dangerous in their raw state. Lightly cooked they become much more palatable. But go too far – cook them too long at too high a temperature – and you create substances known as heterocyclic amines (HCAs) and polycyclic aromatic hydrocarbons (PAHs) which, in sufficient quantity, can cause cell mutations and cancer.

The best advice, then, is: *always eat some raw foods every day.*

And, when cooking, if appropriate: *lightly steam.*

An a–z of longevity wonderfoods

ALMONDS

Almonds can reduce the likelihood of heart attacks. For vegans, they're also a useful source of calcium.

How does it work?

Almonds can lower cholesterol; the high vitamin E content helps keep arteries clear.

How much should I eat?

About 20 nuts a day (25 g/1 oz) will provide almost half the RDA for vitamin E, as well as 20 per cent of the RDA for magnesium and around 5 per cent of your calcium needs.

AVOCADO

Avocados can prevent free radicals entering the bloodstream from the digestive tract.

How does it work?

Avocados contain an antioxidant known as glutathione.

How much should I eat?

One avocado eaten with a high-fat meal will prevent a lot of free radical damage – but don't eat high-fat meals very often.

BARLEY

On average, around 80 per cent of your cholesterol (see box on p. 20) is actually manufactured by your body and only around 20 per cent comes from your food. So cutting back on cholesterol-rich foods can only achieve so much. What you really need to do is slow down your own cholesterol factory. Barley can do that.

How does it work?

Cholesterol is manufactured in the liver. A substance in barley deactivates an enzyme essential to the production of 'bad' LDL cholesterol without lowering 'good' HDL cholesterol.

How much should I eat?

Eating a cupful of barley every day (barley flour is a convenient way) can depress 'bad' LDL cholesterol by about 15 per cent. Barley also fights cancer and improves bowel function.

Insight

Cholesterol is a yellow fat that can clog up your arteries. Eating lots of saturated fat in meat and dairy products can send it soaring. In one experiment, people who got 10 per cent of their energy from saturated fat had 13 per cent lower cholesterol than those who derived 40 per cent of their energy from saturated fat (a not uncommon amount in the West).

But cholesterol is not a simple issue. It turns out there are 'good' and 'bad' forms. The 'good' cholesterol is high-density lipoprotein (HDL) and the 'bad' is low-density lipoprotein (LDL). LDL is responsible for depositing dangerous plaque on the walls of your arteries. HDL, by contrast, acts like a kind of policeman, rounding up the LDL and taking it to your liver where it's rendered harmless.

The following foods can improve the ratio of HDL to LDL and/or help protect your arteries: almonds, apples, avocados, barley, beans, carrots, fish, garlic, grapefruit, oats, olive oil, onions, red wine, vitamins beta carotene, C and E, walnuts, whole grains.

BERRIES

All the berries: blackberries, blueberries, cranberries, raspberries, strawberries and so on – fight cancer.

How does it work?

Berries are high in antioxidants, especially vitamin C. Cranberries and blueberries also fight urinary infections.

How much should I eat?

As much as you like.

BRAZIL NUTS

Brazil nuts help fight heart disease, cancer, arthritis, depression and a failing immune system.

How does it work?

Brazil nuts contain more selenium than any other food and about 2,500 times more selenium than any other nut. Selenium, one of the eight essential trace minerals, is not only an antioxidant but also facilitates the production of glutathione peroxidase, which, like selenium, combats free radicals.

How much should I eat?

You want to aim for 100–200 mcg of selenium a day, which translates as:

▶ *two freshly shelled Brazil nuts, or*
▶ *six ready shelled Brazil nuts.*

Insight

Selenium is actually toxic in large doses so don't exceed the above quantities. A fungus that can grow on the nuts is carcinogenic. Brazil nuts imported into Europe are carefully screened for the fungus but, for safety, don't eat any that are yellow inside – the correct colour is pale ivory.

BROCCOLI

Broccoli is an anti-ageing powerhouse. Eating broccoli regularly is associated with lower rates of cardiovascular disease, lung cancer and colon cancer.

How does it work?

Broccoli is absolutely packed with beneficial nutrients, including the antioxidants vitamin C, beta carotene, sulforaphane, quercetin and glutathione. It also contains calcium (a cupful of cooked broccoli supplies around one fifth of your daily needs) and chromium, which helps regulate blood sugar.

How much should I eat?

Aim to have a portion of broccoli a couple of times a week, raw or only lightly cooked.

CABBAGE

Regular cabbage eaters have less stomach and colon cancer and also less breast cancer.

How does it work?

Cabbage is packed with antioxidants. One called indole-3-carbinol has the ability to destroy a particular kind of oestrogen that's associated with breast cancer. Like broccoli, a cupful of cooked cabbage can also supply around one-fifth of your daily calcium needs.

How much should I eat?

At least once a week have a substantial helping, raw or lightly cooked.

CARROTS

In various studies, carrots have been shown to:

- ▶ *lower blood cholesterol*
- ▶ *reduce the risk of stroke*
- ▶ *fight cancer*
- ▶ *protect eyesight.*

How does it work?

Carrots contain beta carotene, an extremely powerful antioxidant.

How much should I eat?

Eat a couple of medium-sized carrots every day – you'll actually absorb more of the beta carotene if they're *lightly* cooked rather than raw.

GARLIC

Not so long ago most North Europeans and Americans would have wrinkled their noses at the very thought of garlic. Now we're all used to its judicious use with pasta sauces. But most people still aren't getting enough. Garlic:

- ▶ *boosts the immune system*
- ▶ *is an antibiotic*
- ▶ *fights cancer*
- ▶ *thins the blood and dissolves blood clots*
- ▶ *lowers blood pressure*
- ▶ *lowers cholesterol*
- ▶ *improves the circulation (which is possibly the reason for its reputation as a sex stimulant).*

Researchers at the University of Hanover, testing the effect of garlic on high cholesterol, discovered that garlic also boosts mood and reduces anxiety, irritability and fatigue.

How does it work?

Allicin, the chemical that gives garlic its distinctive smell, and which is created when it is either cut or crushed, is certainly one of the key ingredients.

How much should I eat?

The more the better. Try working your way up to a couple of cloves a day (one of them raw).

GRAPEFRUIT (AND ORANGES)

Citrus fruits, especially the pith (the white stuff):

- *lower cholesterol*
- *fight cancer*
- *fight the build-up of plaque in the arteries.*

How does it work?

At least some of the benefit comes from the pectin, a substance well known to jam makers for its ability to solidify the product, but there are other chemicals involved, including vitamin C.

How much should I eat?

Have a citrus fruit every day, and be sure to include the pith. When you eat grapefruit don't put sugar on it.

OATS

As we saw in the case of Mrs Meilleur, oats have a number of beneficial properties. They:

- *lower 'bad' LDL cholesterol and increase 'good' HDL cholesterol*
- *help avoid constipation*
- *protect against diverticulitis and haemorrhoids*
- *help fight certain viruses and cancer in the digestive tract*
- *help regulate blood sugar and insulin*
- *have anti-inflammatory properties*
- *are high in calcium.*

How does it work?

The main cholesterol-improving effect seems to be due to a gummy fibre called beta glucans.

How much should I eat?

A bowl of porridge or oat-based muesli every day.

OLIVE OIL

Ah, the Mediterranean diet! Nowadays we all know about it and one of the key ingredients, of course, is olive oil. On the island of Crete they consume more olive oil per head than any other people on Earth and enjoy some of the world's lowest death rates from heart disease and cancer. Olive oil:

- *lowers 'bad' LDL cholesterol while raising 'good' HDL cholesterol*
- *thins the blood*
- *lowers blood pressure*
- *reduces the risk of heart attack*
- *fights cancer**
- *lowers the risk of death from almost all diseases.*

*Note: In a study led by Dr Alan Kristal of the US Public Health Sciences Division, not only saturated fats but also monounsaturated fats such as olive oil were associated with an increased risk of advanced prostate cancer. There was no association with polyunsaturated fats.

How does it work?

Olive oil contains around a thousand different chemicals and while they haven't all yet been studied it's clear that they're mostly beneficial. Olive oil is largely monounsaturated fat (about 70 per cent) which improves the ratio of LDL to HDL cholesterol. It's also an anticoagulant and contains antioxidants, including vitamin E.

How much should I eat?

At least one tablespoon (15 ml) a day but preferably four or five (60–75 ml), instead of (not in addition to) saturated fats and trans fats. Use it on bread, as a salad dressing and for cooking.

OMEGA-3 FATTY ACIDS

There are many different kinds of fats in food and most of them are 'bad guys', as we've already seen, because of their free radical content. Omega-3 fatty acids, on the other hand, are the 'good guys'.

The key differences between omega-6s and omega-3s are these:

▶ *Omega-6s cause inflammation, constrict blood vessels, encourage blood platelets to stick together and form rigid cell membranes.*
▶ *Omega-3s reduce inflammation, dilate blood vessels, deter blood platelets from sticking together and form flexible cell membranes.*

For optimum functioning you want flexible cell membranes, that is, omega-3s. But in the modern diet, omega-6s outweigh omega-3s at least ten times over. Although omega-6s are essential, that ratio is thought to be too great. Most nutritionists believe it should be not more than 4:1 and preferably close to 1:1. That means finding sources in which omega-3 far *exceeds* omega-6, in order to balance the omega-6 in the rest of the diet (corn oil, for example, contains 46 times more omega-6 than omega-3).

Oily fish provide one solution, especially salmon, swordfish and halibut – two to three portions a week will easily provide your needs. However, there is concern over the high levels of toxins in some fish as well as the environmental impact of overfishing.

Flaxseed (linseed) oil is one alternative, containing about three times more omega-3 than omega-6. However, it's in the form of alpha-linolenic acid (ALA), while the body needs its omega-3 in the form

of eicosapentanoic acid (EPA) and docosahexaenoic acid (DHA).
DHA is particularly good stuff, essential for the development of the
brain, nerves and eyes in infancy, and possibly protective against
heart disease, blood pressure, arteriosclerosis, rheumatoid arthritis,
cardiac arrhythmias, anxiety, depression and, in the elderly, memory
loss. A study published in 2010 suggested that high levels of DHA/
EPA might help maintain the length of telomeres on chromosomes,
the shortening of which has been linked to ageing by some scientists
(see Chapter 1). And as if that weren't enough, brain cells with
membranes rich in DHA seem to communicate more quickly
with one another than those with membranes rich in other fats.
Fortunately, the body can make the conversion between ALA and
DHA but at a rate that's believed to range from 20 per cent in young
women down to just 5 per cent in older men. So, effectively, the
omega-6:omega-3 ratio varies, in broad terms, between 2:1 and 6:1,
rather than 1:3. That's okay, but it's far from ideal.

How much flaxseed oil do you need? The European Food Safety
Authority recommends 250 mg of EPA/DHA while the American
Heart Association is looking at 500 mg of EPA/DHA. Allowing for
the conversion, that means between 1.25 g and 10 g of ALA. Given
that flaxseed is roughly 55 per cent ALA, you'll need 20 g or one
and a half tablespoons per person per day to be on the safe side.

That's easily done. Simply use flaxseed oil on bread or toast in
place of butter or margarine, and in salad dressings. Don't cook
with it. Other plant oils containing omega-3, but in smaller
quantities or in less beneficial proportions, include rapeseed
(canola), soy and walnut.

Insight

All vegetable oils should be kept in the fridge once open (and
stored in a dark place before opening), but this applies all the
more so to flaxseed oil, which oxidizes very rapidly. Oxidized
oil is no longer beneficial – in fact, it's harmful. Aim to buy
bottles you can use in about a week (for one person that
would be 250 ml/9 fl oz).

ONIONS

Onions have been used as a medicine for thousands of years, and
for very good reason. They:

- *are antibiotics*
- *boost 'good' HDL cholesterol*
- *thin the blood*
- *may have anti-cancer properties*
- *regulate blood sugar.*

How does it work?

One of the mechanisms is the suppression of an enzyme that
promotes thromboxane, which causes blood to become sticky.
Onions also contain diphenylamine which lowers blood sugar.

How much should I eat?

As little as a tablespoon of cooked onions served with a high fat
meal will keep 'bad' LDL cholesterol in check. But raw onion
is best. The white and yellow varieties are more potent than the
milder red against LDL cholesterol but the red seems to be higher
in the antioxidant quercetin.

PUMPKIN SEEDS

These flat, dark green seeds are particularly important for men
because they appear to combat benign prostatic hypertrophy
(BPH) – enlargement of the prostate gland. They're also high
in various useful minerals and vitamins including magnesium
and zinc.

How does it work?

That's not quite clear, but it seems BHP is linked with the stimulation of prostate cells by testosterone and its conversion product dihydrotestosterone (DHT), and that the pumpkin seeds somehow interfere with this mechanism.

How much should I eat?

A good handful a day.

RED WINE/GRAPES

In one 13-year study of 12,000 men by the Imperial Cancer Research Fund, moderate drinkers lived two years longer than non-drinkers. Wine, especially red wine, seems to have the most benefits because it:

- ▶ *reduces the clogging of arteries*
- ▶ *lowers the risk of heart attacks*
- ▶ *lowers the risk of strokes*
- ▶ *dilates blood vessels*
- ▶ *improves cognitive function.*

How does it work?

The beneficial effects of red wine has been attributed to resveratrol, which has been shown to extend life in mice, possibly by activating a gene called SIRT-1 (the 'survival gene' that also seems to be activated in calorie restriction as described on pages 35–38). The plant produces resveratrol in response to attack by bacteria and fungi. Because of that, it's impossible to predict how much resveratrol there will be – you may well be drinking wine in which the proportion is too low to have an effect. Some scientists think procyanidins could be the 'magic' ingredient, and that's possible, but you'll get a much larger quantity from apples. Still others think it's the alcohol itself, in which case any source would do. Even if it doesn't extend life, alcohol has the popular effect of increasing dopamine in the brain (a chemical that causes happiness and euphoria) by indirectly inhibiting neurons that would otherwise suppress it. Most likely, red wine simply has a lucky combination of many things, at least some of which you can get without the alcohol by eating red grapes and drinking red grape juice.

How much should I drink/eat?

Red grapes have been found to contain between 0.15 mg and 0.8 mg of resveratrol per 100 g, while Spanish red wine has been found to contain 0.3 mg–1.9 mg per glass of 150 ml, and red grape juice about one-third less on average. If you want to get your resveratrol from wine (assuming it *is* the 'magic' ingredient) you'll have to strike a balance between positive and negative consequences (see below for side effects). Although the safe 'official' *maximum* amount of alcohol is considered to be three units a day/21 a week for a man and two units a day/14 a week for a woman, *those levels are certainly too high for optimum health and longevity*. A study of a million middle-aged women conducted by a team under Naomi E. Allen at the Cancer Epidemiology Unit at the University of Oxford concluded that drinking more than one to two units *a week* increased the risk of a wide range of cancers. And a study by the French National Cancer Institute concluded that it was *daily* consumption, even of small quantities, that was the most dangerous. For more on this see Chapter 8. The best advice is to drink your wine with a meal, maybe three times a week, and have no more than one or two glasses if a man and one glass if a woman (or either sex if aged over 65).

Any side effects?

Plenty. Heavy drinking increases the risk of high blood pressure, strokes, some cancers and cirrhosis of the liver. Some people keep increasing their intake to overcome their tolerance and end up addicted. Addiction can lead to dementia, psychosis and depression. Under the influence of alcohol people are more prone to accidents, violence and suicide. So stick to the levels above and drink red grape juice or eat red grapes in addition.

SOYBEANS

All beans are beneficial but soybeans are particularly powerful. They:

▸ *lower cholesterol*
▸ *fight certain cancers, especially in the stomach*
▸ *regulate blood sugar*
▸ *combat post-menopausal symptoms*
▸ *combat osteoporosis, because of their high calcium content*
▸ *improve bowel function*
▸ *combat gallstones.*

How does it work?

For a start, soybeans contain lots of antioxidants, including genistein: a powerful cancer fighter, especially in the breast and prostate. They also contain the amino acids glycine and arginine, which reduce insulin – high insulin is linked with ageing.

How much should I eat?

The latest research suggests the benefits come from eating whole soybeans, while soy supplements and purified forms of soy might actually be harmful. So stick with the beans, soybean sprouts, tofu, miso and tempeh three or four times a week.

TEA

Real tea – the leaves of **Camellia sinensis** – will help you live longer. Tea:

▸ *fights cancer*
▸ *lowers cholesterol*

- ▸ *lowers the risk of heart disease*
- ▸ *lowers the risk of stroke*
- ▸ *protects arteries*
- ▸ *dissolves blood clots*
- ▸ *protects teeth and gums.*

How does it work?

Tea contains plenty of antioxidants such as quercetin and catechins, as well as compounds that fight harmful bacteria in the mouth.

How much should I drink?

The beneficial effects start after about 30 minutes for green tea and 50 minutes for black tea. But after about 80 minutes the effects wear off – so you need to drink several cups a day to keep up the antioxidant levels in your blood. The Chinese and Japanese drink tea with meals – which is a very good way of neutralizing any carcinogens in food. Brew for three minutes to maximize antioxidants.

TOMATOES

Tomatoes are becoming more and more known for their ability to ward off prostate cancer. But they have other benefits as well. They:

- ▸ *prolong mental agility in the elderly*
- ▸ *fight cancer of the pancreas, cervix and digestive tract, as well as the prostate.*

How does it work?

An important antioxidant called lycopene is present in significant quantities in tomatoes (and watermelons, and in small amounts in apricots). Tomatoes also contain p-coumaric acid and chlorogenic acid which suppress cancer-causing nitrosamines.

How much should I eat?

Neither cooking nor processing destroys lycopene so you can take your tomatoes fresh, as juice or in sauces. You should have tomatoes in some form every day – the more concentrated the better.

YOGHURT

A tremendous folklore has long surrounded yoghurt and scientists have now proven much of it true. Yoghurt:

▶ *combats intestinal infections, including diarrhoea*
▶ *improves bowel function*
▶ *protects against ulcers*
▶ *boosts the immune system*
▶ *kills harmful bacteria*
▶ *fights cancer.*

How does it work?

Yoghurt's medicinal qualities seem to be due to bacteria of the lactobacilli family (L. acidophilus seems to be the most beneficial of all). Make sure your yoghurt is live (that is, the bacteria haven't been killed by pasteurization).

How much should I eat?

Aim for at least a wine glass full a day. If you're a vegan, eat soya yoghurt – the benefits won't be identical but they will be significant.

SLOW RELEASE FOODS

Foods that are high on the Glycaemic Index (GI) release their energy quickly and soon leave you in need of another 'hit'. Meanwhile, your blood sugar yo-yos, which is unhealthy. It's much better to favour foods that are low on the GI. Because they release their energy slowly, you don't feel the need to snack between meals and your blood sugar remains stable.

The Glycaemic Index gives the number 100 to pure glucose and assigns other nutrients a number relative to that. High sugar levels are related to heart disease, high insulin, high cholesterol, hypertension and colo-rectal cancer. For many foods, you can guess fairly easily whether they're high or low on the Index but there are also a few surprises.

Some high GI foods		*Some low GI foods*	
White rice	88	Brown rice	55
Baked potato	85	Sweet potato	54
Corn Flakes	84	Peas	48
Watermelon	72	All-Bran	42
Carrot	71	Spaghetti	41
White bread	70	Spaghetti al dente	37
Croissant	67	Chickpeas	33
Blueberry muffin	59	Lentils	29
		Peach	28
		Kidney beans	27
		Barley	25
		Grapefruit	25
		Peanuts	14

Insight

Foods that (when appropriate) are 'undercooked' are slightly lower on the Index than if they're well cooked (see spaghetti in the above table).

Crash diets

Crash diets are almost always a waste of time. Yes, you may lose weight but you'll probably put it back on again within one to five years. Most people do. Unfortunately, that's the reality. The only sensible way to control your weight is to develop healthy eating habits *for life*.

Just think about it for a moment. If, from the age of 20, you put on as little as 1 kg (2.2 lb) a year – an almost unnoticeable amount – you could be an unaesthetic 10 kg (22 lb) overweight by 30, a worrying 20 kg (44 lb) overweight by 40 and a frightening 30 kg (66 lb) overweight by 50. But all you have to do each day to avoid that happening is cut out one pudding, or equivalent, or walk for 45 minutes.

> The moment you notice you're going above your ideal weight either cut back the calories or increase the exercise.

Of course, that's not much help to you if you are already overweight. But if you've made up your mind to do something about it then, above all, be patient. Don't even contemplate a crash diet. Instead aim to lose no more than 1–2 kg (2.2–4.4 lb) a month, by healthy eating.

In other words, if you're around 6 kg (roughly one stone) over your optimum weight then aim to get back to your ideal in three to six months. If you're, say, 13 kg overweight (roughly two stone) aim to get down to your optimum in six months to a year. And then *continue with your new, healthy way of eating for life.*

Earlier in this chapter, you've seen what foods are good for you and which to avoid or cut down on. All the good foods are tasty and enjoyable so there's no 'pain' involved. At first you may well miss some of the food you've been used to. That's perfectly normal. Your taste buds, your sense of smell, your body and, above all, your mind all need time to adapt. But after a few months – it does take a while – you'll probably lose your appetite for your old way of eating. *The secret is never to get hungry.* When you're hungry your willpower is low and you are more likely to give in to an urge for a 'quick hit' of sugar or fat. And the way to avoid hunger is to eat 'slow release' complex carbohydrates.

Restrict calories, live longer

Restricting calories is something subtly different from dieting. The evidence is that people who consume below the 'normal' level of calories and who are right at the bottom end of the 'normal' weight range for their height live longer. For example, compared with the heaviest, a middle-aged man who restricts calories so as to remain among the slimmest for his age will, on average, live 40 per cent longer.

The first experiments carried out were on animals. Among those experimenting was Dr Roy Walford, who found that keeping mice on a restricted diet not only almost doubled their lifespan but preserved mental agility – calorie-deprived three-year-old mice performed maze tests like youngsters (see Chapter 5 for more on keeping your brain young). And there's been plenty of anecdotal evidence to suggest the same is true with humans. Now we more or less have the proof. A 27-year study of 19,000 Harvard graduates found that those who were 20 per cent below the average weight – and therefore eating fewer calories – lived the longest. Unfortunately, Dr Walford himself died at the age of 79, well short of his target of 120. Does that disprove his theory? Probably not, because he died from amyotrophic lateral sclerosis, also known as Lou Gehrig's disease. He himself believed that due to calorie restriction he survived much longer than he would otherwise have done.

> A rule of thumb is that you need to stay at the weight you were when you were 25 (assuming you weren't overweight then).

How can this be? In fact, some of the mechanisms at work are perfectly logical and predictable while others are more mysterious. For one thing, calorie restriction may activate a gene called SIRT-1, the so-called 'survival gene' that would have helped our ancestors endure long periods of famine. What's more, the less you eat:

▸ *the fewer free radicals you produce*
▸ *the lower your temperature*
▸ *the lower your blood sugar and insulin levels*
▸ *the lower your cholesterol*
▸ *the lower your blood pressure*
▸ *the lower your metabolic rate*
▸ *the more antioxidant enzymes you produce*

▶ *the more vigorous your immune system*
▶ *the more slowly precancerous cells reproduce.*

Calorie restriction (or CR as it is known to scientists) is, in fact, the only *proven* method of extending the human lifespan. However, recent evidence suggests it may not be so much a question of restricting calories as restricting protein (see *Is it worth giving up meat?* on page 39).

Optimum weights for living longer

Height	Men	Women
158 cm/5′ 2″	48–57 kg (105–125 lb)	44–52 kg (97–114 lb)
163 cm/5′ 4″	51–60 kg (112–132 lb)	46–55 kg (101–121 lb)
168 cm/5′ 6″	53–63 kg (117–139 lb)	49–58 kg (108–128 lb)
173 cm/5′ 8″	57–66 kg (125–145 lb)	52–61 kg (114–134 lb)
178 cm/5′ 10″	61–70 kg (134–154 lb)	55–64 kg (121–141 lb)
183 cm/6′	64–74 kg (141–163 lb)	59–68 kg (130–150 lb)

Note: If you're small boned you should be at the bottom end of the scale; only if you're large boned should you be at the top of the scale. If your height lies between the heights in the table then your target weight should similarly lie between the target weights in the table.

It's important to emphasize that the benefits come from calorie (or possibly protein) restriction, not low weight itself. Weight is only an indicator that, indeed, your intake is low. Keeping slim through exercise is not the same thing – although exercise has other very valuable benefits. If you want to work out exactly what CR means for you, simply multiply the healthy weight (in kilograms) for your height and build by 24, to arrive at the calories you would require to maintain that weight if you weren't doing manual work or exercising. Then take 75 per cent of that figure. That gives you the number of calories you can consume each day on CR. For example, a woman who is at her correct weight of 60 kg would be allowed:

$60 \times 24 \times 75\% = 1{,}440 \times 75\% = 1{,}080$ calories per day.

That's extremely harsh, especially bearing in mind that the figure doesn't go up, no matter how much exercise you're doing. And although those on CR will, *on average*, live longer, a given individual may not. There are downsides, too, such as loss of muscle, loss of physical strength and endurance, and loss of bone density (which could lead to fractures). So this is something that requires very careful thought.

If you *do* opt for calorie restriction:

▶ *Make the adjustment over a period of one to two years: your body needs time to adjust and rapid weight loss could actually be harmful.*
▶ *Make sure you avoid 'empty calories' and have only nutrient-dense foods that provide all the vitamins and minerals you need.*

Insight

My own opinion is that CR is just too extreme and detracts from the ability to enjoy life. If, like me, you relish physical activities (jogging, swimming, cycling, snowboarding...) you'll find you just can't achieve as much on CR. The study of Harvard graduates quoted above suggests that keeping very slim but without CR is a good compromise.

Is it worth giving up meat?

A 21-year study by the German Cancer Research Centre at Heidelberg found no significant difference in the life expectancy of vegetarians as compared with *health-conscious, moderate* meat eaters. It seems the advantage over the general population may be conferred by a high intake of plant foods, whether accompanied by meat or not.

However, there's no doubt that a *high* consumption of saturated fat in meat and dairy is associated with a shorter life. For example, a study by Professor Richard Shekelle at the University of Texas Health Science Center in Houston found that those eating 700 mg or more of cholesterol a day lived, on average, three years less than those with low cholesterol consumption. Dr Pramil Singh at the Loma Linda University School of Public Health, California, led a review of six studies and came to a similar conclusion. His team determined that eating meat less than once a week resulted in an average increase in life expectancy of three years and 219 days.

But what about giving up animal products altogether? Dr Richard C. Grandison and his colleagues at University College, London, discovered that fruit flies (*Drosophila*) on CR did indeed live longer but that the advantage was lost if extra amino acids (which make proteins) were given. That proved to be the case even though overall calories remained the same. The densest sources of protein are meat and cheese which come in around 25 g of protein per 100 g.

No one really knows how much protein a human adult needs but a widely-accepted figure is 0.75 g per kg of body weight per day, which is 56 g for a 75 kg (11.5 stone) man and 48 g for a 64 kg (10-stone) woman. Restricting protein would be quite difficult for a meat-eater. To give you an idea, a generous steak would alone give a man about twice

(Contd)

his daily protein requirement. A vegan, on the other hand, would struggle to meet it.

So you don't have to give up animal products entirely to gain benefits, but it seems that if you do you may get a longevity boost from protein restriction as well. What's more, by reducing or eliminating your consumption of animal products you'll certainly find it easier to restrict calories and lose weight. A 100 g (3.5 oz) portion of roast sirloin, for example, contains some 380 calories, and cheddar cheese is the same, whereas a 100 g (3.5 oz) carrot contains about 25.

If you do decide to give up meat, bear in mind that being vegetarian or vegan doesn't automatically guarantee a healthy diet. There are unhealthy vegan and vegetarian regimes, too. The secret of living entirely without animal products is variety. Every day you should have:

▶ *fresh and dried fruits*
▶ *vegetables, including pulses*
▶ *whole grains*
▶ *nuts*
▶ *seeds.*

If you're a vegan it's also vitally important that you get adequate vitamin B12 from fortified foods such as yeast extracts or from a supplement. Sufficient vitamin B12 is extremely difficult to obtain from plants alone.

Insight

People often tell me they 'don't like vegetables'. But taste is very much a matter of conditioning. There nothing an Inuit likes better than some nice raw blubber. It's a question of what you get used to. Over a few months I guarantee you'll come to love vegetables and fruit as much as you now love steak. Another reason people give me for not cutting down or cutting out meat is that they won't have enough energy. Well, I've run a marathon as a vegan and in a perfectly respectable time – energy, I assure you, is not a problem.

The live-longer meal planner

The suggestions below incorporate all the ideas in this book for optimum longevity through nutrition. If they're very different from your current style of eating then don't rush to change. The body – and the mind – takes time to adjust. Give yourself from a few months to a year to make the transition.

SEVEN BREAKFAST SUGGESTIONS

It's very important not to feel hungry at any time, otherwise you'll be tempted into a quick-fix, high-sugar snack. A good breakfast is your first line of defence and should set you up for the whole morning. Try any of the following:

1 Muesli *(see box on page 42).*
2 Porridge: *Eat unsweetened with a touch of salt. A standard portion is just 100 calories so you can eat as much as you like.*
3 Lightly stewed fresh fruit with ginger: *Mix according to taste and season – apples, assorted berries, cherries, grapefruit, kiwi, oranges, peaches, pears, plums... whatever you fancy. Top the whole lot off with some yoghurt and a sprinkling of seeds and chopped nuts. A full bowl will probably amount to around 300 calories.*
4 Whole grain multi-cereal toast (1): *Moisten with flaxseed oil and top with a smear of yeast extract, chopped raw garlic, tofu, sliced tomatoes and a garnish of rocket. Two slices will be around 300 calories.*
5 Whole grain multi-cereal toast (2): *Moisten with flaxseed oil and top with guacamole, mixed seeds, crushed nuts and a garnish of watercress. Two slices will be around 350 calories.*

6   Whole grain multi-cereal toast (3): *Moisten with flaxseed oil and top with hummus (a spread made of chickpeas, sesame tahini, lemon juice and garlic – also spelt houmous), cumin, mixed seeds, crushed nuts, and a garnish of mustard and cress. Two slices will be around 500 calories.*

7   Whole grain multi-cereal toast (4): *Moisten with olive oil and top with black olive paté, raw chopped garlic, tofu, sliced cucumber and a garnish of beansprouts. Two slices will be around 350 calories.*

'Super-muesli' meals

Some people love muesli and some say they hate it. 'Horse food!', they complain. But muesli isn't just one dish. It's a whole range of dishes. Just as you can have many different pasta meals, so you can enjoy a huge variety of muesli meals. With a little imagination, 'boring' muesli becomes fabulous super-muesli.

And the great thing is that you can eat just about as much of it as you like. A full cereal bowl won't amount to more than about 500 calories and will keep you going for six hours or more. Plus it's extremely versatile. By varying the ingredients you can make it a suitable dish for breakfast, lunch, or even dinner, and stop it ever becoming monotonous. One super-muesli meal every day can give you a substantial number of the wonderfoods you need.

Ingredients (for one person):

An unsweetened muesli base
Two or three shelled Brazil nuts for selenium, cut into
     manageable pieces
Half a dozen walnuts, for omega-3
A small handful of pumpkin seeds for zinc and (for men)
     the prostate

Any other raw nuts and seeds you fancy
A small handful of raisins or sultanas
Fruit according to season and taste: for example, half
*   a banana, half an apple, some grapefruit segments,*
*   a kiwi and a handful of assorted berries*
Orange juice
A 125 g (4.5 oz) tub of yoghurt (soya yoghurt for vegans).

Method:

Put the dry ingredients into a bowl and cover with orange juice. Do this at least ten minutes beforehand – longer if you like your cereals soft and your dried fruits plumped up with the juice. Then add the fruit in pieces and top the whole thing off with the yoghurt.

SEVEN LUNCH SUGGESTIONS

If you eat dinner at around, say, 8 p.m., you need a lunch that's going to keep you going for about six hours. Otherwise, you'll be strongly tempted towards a quick and unhealthy sugar hit. That will drive up your calorie intake without providing any very beneficial nutrients. So lunch needs to be something substantial.

1 Muesli: *an excellent choice (see box).*
2 Dips: Prepare *fingers of toasted whole grain multi-cereal bread, apple, broccoli, carrot, celery, cucumber, red and green peppers (all raw) together with a variety of dips such as alioli (mayonnaise-like sauce made with garlic and olive oil: see box on page 45), guacamole, hummus, romesco sauce, spicy tomato sauce and yoghurt. Eat as much as you like (it will be hard to exceed 500 calories).*
3 Stuffed cabbage leaves: *Steam the cabbage leaves to soften, then fill with a mixture of cooked brown rice, pine nuts or pistachio nuts, rehydrated raisins and chopped garlic. Place in a baking dish, top with a tomato sauce and heat through in the oven.*

4   Super-salad *(see box below)*.

5   Barley grits: *Put the grits (the barley grains hulled and coarsely ground) to soak in water about an hour before they're needed, then drain thoroughly. Toss together with chopped tomatoes, onions, cucumber, garlic, parsley, mint, olive oil and lemon juice to make a tabbouleh (tabbouli).*

6   Fresh vegetable soup, *including brown rice, whole grains and beans.*

7   Open sandwich: *Use whole grain multi-cereal bread as a base, moisten with flaxseed oil and top with wonderfoods. For example: coleslaw made from shredded cabbage, onion and carrot in alioli (see box right), tofu and a sprinkling of pumpkin seeds.*

Super-salad

Forget everything you thought you knew about salads and how dull they are and how you're always starving afterwards. The super-salad is different, a complete meal in itself.

What makes it super is the number of ingredients. Aim to incorporate at least a dozen and preferably 20 or more. Look for unusual combinations of taste, texture and colour. Always have some salad leaves, perhaps two or three types, and then make a selection from (for example): apple, avocado, beansprouts, beetroot, broad beans, broccoli, carrot, celery, chickpeas, cucumber, garlic, grapes, kidney beans, lentils, mango, melon, mushrooms, olives, onion, papaya, peas, pears, peppers, pineapple, pistachio nuts, pomegranate, potatoes (boiled and cooled), pumpkin seeds, raisins, rice (brown, cooked and cooled), sultanas, soya beans, sunflower seeds, sweetcorn, tofu, tomatoes, walnuts, wholemeal pasta. You're limited only by your imagination.

You'll then need a dressing. Here's one suggestion:

Find a jar with a well-fitting lid and into it put a small glass of olive oil, one-third of a glass of balsamic vinegar, one teaspoon of Dijon mustard, a dash of Tabasco sauce, salt, freshly ground black pepper and chopped garlic to taste. Put on the lid, shake vigorously and, when well mixed, pour over the salad.

Alioli

Alioli is a kind of Spanish mayonnaise made from two wonderfoods: garlic and olive oil. To prepare it at home, crush some peeled garlic cloves in a mortar and when they're the consistency of chewing gum begin adding the olive oil drop by drop while whisking vigorously. The result is a stiff, white pungent and extremely healthy sauce. The easy way is to buy it ready-made.

SEVEN DINNER SUGGESTIONS

Dinner is a meal to eat at leisure with the one you love, with family and with friends. Always try to make it a special occasion. Be sure to include key nutrients that were missed during the day.

1 To begin: *a salad of orange rings, grapefruit rings, raw onion rings and black olives;*
   Followed by: *steamed vegetables (for example potatoes, broccoli, onions, carrots) with tofu chunks, sprinkled with olive oil and balsamic vinegar.*
2 To begin: *leek and cabbage vinaigrette (leeks and strips of cabbage cooked, cooled and served with a vinaigrette dressing);*
   Followed by: *vegetable curry with brown rice.*

3 To begin: *some pa i tomàquet (Catalan favourite: toast – use wholegrain multi-cereal bread – rubbed with raw garlic, tomato and drizzled with olive oil);*
   Followed by: *a super-salad (see box on page 44).*
4 To begin: *Jersulem artichokes sliced thinly and roasted or steamed whole, served with alioli (see box on page 45);*
   Followed by: *ratatouille on a bed of boiled whole grain barley.*
5 To begin: *grated carrot with orange juice and Kalonji black onion seeds;*
   Followed by: *oven-roasted vegetables (for example potatoes, sweet potatoes, aubergine, courgettes, tomatoes, carrots, whole onions, and whole heads of garlic).*
6 To begin: *a selection of crudités (for example raw carrot, celeriac, beetroot, tomatoes and onion, grated, diced or shredded as appropriate, with various sauces and dressings);*
   Followed by: *roast fennel in orange sauce sprinkled with toasted pumpkin seeds.*
7 To begin: *gazpacho (cold tomato and garlic soup served with finely-diced cucumber, red pepper and onion);*
   Followed by: *vegetable paella with brown rice.*

And for a party...
Barbecue of fresh or frozen green asparagus, wild mushrooms, and vegetable kebabs with tofu chunks served with plenty of alioli.

SNACKS

The best thing is not to eat any. The reason is this: it's not so much the main meals that put on the weight and cause the unhealthy spikes in blood sugar as all the extras. One chocolate chip cookie with every cup of tea or coffee during the day could add about 500 calories – the equivalent of an entire extra meal. A single portion of chocolate cake could add the same. Get your main meals right and you won't need them. However, if on occasion you're not able to eat properly and need something to keep you going, opt for low calorie, low to medium GI foods. Here are some suggestions:

- *Raw carrot slices with a dip of hummus or guacamole.*
- *A handful of dried fruits, nuts and seeds.*
- *A handful of pumpkin seeds.*
- *Fresh fruit (a peach is around 40 calories, an orange 50 calories, an apple 60 calories, a banana 100 calories).*
- *Fresh fruit mixed into a bowl of yoghurt.*

DRINKS

How much should you actually drink in a day? The often-heard advice that you need to drink 2 litres (3.5 pints) of water or even more is an exaggeration. If you're having plenty of vegetables and fruits, as recommended here, they'll make a major contribution. Nor is it true that tea and coffee don't count because they're diuretics – you'll still gain by drinking them. The best test is probably the colour of your urine – if it's pale you're drinking enough, if it's yellow you're not.

But you *do* need to drink plenty of water if:

- *you have kidney stones or a tendency to kidney stones*
- *the weather is hot.*

Tea, either black or green, is a great drink. If it's unsweetened and served without milk it's only a calorie or two (the same goes for fruit teas and black coffee). However, a dob of milk could add around 20 calories and a couple of teaspoons of sugar could add a further 40 calories. Multiply that by six cups a day and we're talking a highly significant 360 calories. The answer is to get used to your drinks without sugar and, at least some of the time, without milk.

Fruit juices and vegetable juices are rich in nutrients so they're well worth the 50 calories per wine glass full. Men should aim to drink a glass of tomato juice every day.

Pure alcohol contains 7 calories per gram, which puts it roughly half-way between sugar and pure fat. In real life, that works out at around 50 calories for a measure (25 ml) of gin; 80 calories for a glass (115 ml) of dry red wine; 100 calories for half a pint (284 ml) of normal-strength lager or beer; and 200 calories for half a pint (284 ml) of extra-strength lager or beer. So anyone drinking three glasses of wine is having the equivalent of a light meal while anyone drinking three pints of strong beer is having the equivalent of a banquet.

10 THINGS TO REMEMBER

1 *Eating plenty of the right foods and cutting down on the wrong foods (especially trans-fats, saturated fats, hydrogenated and solidified oils, salt, sugar and processed foods) is proven to extend life.*

2 *Avoid 'empty calories': food that doesn't contain much by way of vitamins and useful minerals.*

3 *Ageing is partly caused by free radical damage to cells.*

4 *Free radicals are associated with a diet high in fat; use monounsaturates and oil that is high in omega-3 wherever possible.*

5 *Antioxidants, present in many fruits and vegetables, combat free radicals.*

6 *Eat some raw food every day – when cooking, lightly steam whenever appropriate.*

7 *'Wonderfoods' include avocados, barley, berries, Brazil nuts, broccoli, cabbage, carrots, citrus fruits, garlic, oats, olive oil, flaxseed oil, onions, pumpkin seeds, red wine, soybeans, tea, tomatoes and yoghurt.*

8 *Choose 'slow release' foods in preference to foods high on the GI index.*

9 *Never crash diet – lose weight gradually through a healthy way of eating for life.*

10 *Calorie restriction (CR) is proven to extend life – cutting down or cutting out animal products is an easy way to reduce calories and has other health benefits, too.*

HOW MUCH LONGER ARE YOU GOING TO LIVE NOW?

▶ *Are you switching to whole foods wherever possible and avoiding processed foods?*

▶ *Are you switching to olive oil for cooking and flaxseed oil for salad dressings?*

▶ *Are you eating some raw food every day?*

▶ *Are you increasing your consumption of the 'wonderfoods'?*

▶ *Are you switching to foods low on the Glycaemic Index (GI)?*

▶ *Have you given up crash diets in favour of a new, healthy way of eating for life?*

▶ *Are you getting your weight down to the level you were at when you were 25 (assuming you weren't overweight then)?*

▶ *Are you cutting down on or even cutting out animal products?*

▶ *If you are cutting out animal products, are you taking a B12 supplement?*

▶ *Are you drinking enough to keep your urine pale?*

Score:

If you answered 'yes' to eight or more questions you're obviously very serious about living longer and are taking the steps that will be rewarded by a significant increase in your life expectancy. Move on to the next chapter.

If you answered 'yes' to between five and seven questions you're well on the way to a better lifestyle. You can also move on to the next chapter but re-read this one from time to time and gradually try to introduce all the recommendations.

If you answered 'yes' to four or fewer questions you certainly want to live longer (who doesn't?) but you're not yet prepared to make the lifestyle commitments to bring that about. It may be that others are undermining your resolve. If that's the case, try to get your partner, family or friends to be more supportive and perhaps join you in your health drive. Work on getting a 'yes' to at least five questions before tackling other chapters.

3

Supplements

In this chapter you will learn:
- *why it's difficult to get the Recommended Dietary Allowance (RDA) for some crucial nutrients*
- *why artificial supplements may be needed*
- *how mega-doses of some vitamins may protect against disease and prolong life.*

By the proper intakes of vitamins and other nutrients and by following a few other healthful practices from youth to middle age on, you can, I believe, extend your life and years of well-being by twenty-five or even thirty-five years.

Dr Linus Pauling

Warning: Nutrition is an extremely complicated subject and you are therefore advised to consult a doctor or qualified nutritionist before taking vitamins or minerals as a supplement. Exercise extreme care if taking both multivitamin/mineral tablets and individual vitamin or mineral tablets – you may end up getting far more of a particular vitamin or mineral than you intended.

The great supplement debate

Just as we all do, Linus Pauling wanted to live a long time. But he had one great advantage over most of us when it came to working out how: he was a scientist. And a pretty accomplished one at that. In 1954 he won the Nobel Prize for chemistry. In 1962 he got another Nobel Prize for peace. And if he hadn't been wrongly pursuing a triple helix rather than the now famous double helix he probably would have had a third Nobel Prize for discovering the structure of DNA.

So when Dr Pauling applied his mind to the knotty little problem of his own longevity (and yours and mine) something interesting was likely to turn up. It did. He called it 'orthomolecular medicine'. And it's been the subject of controversy ever since.

What is this orthomolecular medicine? Well, it's the maintenance of health and the treatment of disease using *substances naturally present in the body*. For general longevity purposes, Dr Pauling took an 'elixir' of these substances every day. It actually consisted of four tablets and a fine crystalline powder. One of the tablets was vitamin A, one was vitamin B complex, one was vitamin E and the fourth was a mineral supplement. As to the powder, it was vitamin C. So the ingredients weren't unusual.

The magic, if magic there was, was in the dose. Dr Pauling took 25,000 IU of vitamin A, five times what was then the Recommended Dietary Allowance (RDA). Of the B vitamins he took around 50 times the RDA. Of vitamin E he took 80 times the RDA. And with regards vitamin C, the vitamin he considered the most important of all, he took an incredible 18 g or 300 times what was then believed to be the proper quantity. In other words, almost a year's worth of vitamin C every single day.

Dr Pauling claimed that vitamin C, a substance involved in a wide range of bodily processes, could boost the immune system, accelerate wound healing and have a powerful effect on numerous problems including the common cold, flu, cardiovascular disease, cancer, allergies, arthritis, periodontal disease, cataracts and glaucoma.

Although he did carry out original research, Dr Pauling didn't so much invent orthomolecular medicine as analyse and compile the pioneering work of many other scientists and doctors using vitamins to treat specific conditions. His contribution was to forge their work into a coherent, unified theory. So Dr Pauling's is far from a lone voice.

The problem is that almost every proof advanced by Dr Pauling has been rebutted by other scientists. And, for the moment, those other scientists are generally the ones the medical establishment supports.

It seems it should be easy to test orthomolecular medicine and pronounce on it one way or the other. But it's actually extremely difficult. To begin with, Dr Pauling's daily dose of vitamin C is nine times higher than the safe maximum recommended by the US National Academy of Sciences. This makes it ethically tricky, although not impossible, for scientists to administer it. Nevertheless, some have.

A study by Dr Ewan Cameron at the Vale of Leven Hospital in Scotland, for example, significantly extended the survival times of terminal cancer patients, using 10 g of vitamin C intravenously for ten days and then by pill. Some survived more than five years (a 'cure' in statistical terms) while none of the controls did. Similar results were obtained by the Fukuoka Torikai Hospital in Japan, using average doses of 29 g. However, the mechanism of ultra-high doses seems not to be that they're healthy but that they're toxic – more toxic to cancer cells than normal cells. For a discussion of this see *Vitamin C* on pages 72–74.

Many doctors simply argue the common-sense view that since human beings evolved *without* vitamin supplements then our bodies must be designed to provide us with a natural lifespan *without* vitamin supplements. Well, that sounds pretty logical. Case proven. No third Nobel Prize for Dr Pauling.

But hang on a minute! Do we actually want to settle for a 'natural' lifespan? Surely not. Yes, a normal diet may be fine for a normal life but if you want to live an abnormal life – much longer than you otherwise would have done – perhaps you need an *abnormal* diet. In other words, you need to take in far higher quantities of certain vitamins and minerals than are easily achieved from food alone.

One test would be Dr Pauling's age when he died. But, unfortunately, Dr Pauling left us a conundrum, not a proof. If he were still alive today he'd be well on his way to claiming the title of the world's oldest man. Or if he'd died decades earlier in, say, 1970, his detractors might have permitted themselves a little private smirk. But he didn't do anything so convenient for science. He died in 1994 at the age of 93 of prostate cancer, something he shouldn't have got.

But before you decide that Dr Pauling disproved his own orthomolecular medicine, reflect that the life expectancy for an American male when Dr Pauling was born was a mere 48 years. Dr Pauling very nearly lived twice as long. And he himself was convinced he had prolonged his own life by 20 years.

So who was right? We simply don't know. There's evidence both ways. You'll have to make your own decision. But if the case for megavitamins has not been generally accepted we do know this for sure: *Older people can't easily obtain even the RDA for all vitamins from food alone.*

The fact is that as we age, our ability to absorb certain vitamins and minerals from food diminishes. Dr Robert Russell, a researcher at Tufts University in the USA says that from around age 65 onwards, almost nobody gets the RDA of a whole range of nutrients, simply because older bodies can't extract them efficiently from food.

In other words: *Supplements are essential for older people to bring them up to at least the RDA.*

What's an RDA?

In Britain, the initials RDA stand for Recommended Daily Amount, the quantity of a nutrient that is officially considered to be adequate for health. In the USA the initials stand for Recommended Dietary Allowance. The US values have been reviewed in the last few years and, at the same time, the Food and Nutrition Board of the US National Academy of Sciences also introduced an Adequate Intake (AI), an Estimated Average Requirement (EAR) and a Tolerable Upper Intake Level (UL).

Some anti-ageing scientists consider the RDAs set for certain vitamins, both in Britain and the USA, to be far too low. They argue that the RDAs may be sufficient to prevent diseases such as scurvy and beriberi but they're not sufficient to play a role in prolonging life.

Take **vitamin B12**, for example. One study suggests that more than half of all Westerners are deficient after the age of 60. And the older you get, the worse the deficiency becomes. Another study showed that 20 per cent of Americans aged over 60, and 40 per cent aged over 80 didn't secrete enough stomach acid to absorb it. For those people, supplementation is essential. In extreme cases, doctors – ordinary, mainstream doctors – give the vitamin by injection. Interestingly, one of the symptoms of B12 deficiency is dementia and, following the injections, patients have quickly recovered their mental faculties. Some experts believe that at least a fifth of those diagnosed with Alzheimer's are actually suffering from easily reversible B12 deficiency.

Or consider **calcium**. If you're an older woman it's quite likely your doctor has prescribed a supplement to combat osteoporosis (see pages 61–63 for the latest research). Or if you're a woman who suffers heavy periods your doctor may have prescribed an iron supplement.

So supplements are mainstream. In principle, they're nothing new or revolutionary. The only argument is over which supplements and what quantity.

Dr Pauling's 'elixir'

The table below compares the US Recommended Dietary Allowance (RDA) for adults* with Dr Pauling's recommendations:

	RDA	Dr Pauling's recommendation
Vitamin C	90 mg	1,000–18,000 mg
Vitamin E	22.5 IU	800 IU
Vitamin A	5000 IU	20,000–40,000 IU
Vitamin D	600 IU	800 IU
B1 (Thiamin)	1.2 mg	50–100 mg
B2 (Riboflavin)	1.3 mg	50–100 mg
B3 (Niacin)	16 mg	300–600 mg
B6 (Pyridoxine)	1.7 mg	50–100 mg
B12	2.4 mcg	100–200 mg
Folic Acid (Folate)	400 mcg	400–800 mcg
Pantothenic Acid	5.0 mg	100–200 mg

IU = International Unit

*Where the RDA is different for men and women or for different age groups, the table gives the highest figure.

VITAMIN AND MINERAL SUPPLEMENTS IN DETAIL

There are two stages, then, in vitamin and mineral supplementation:

1 *Supplementation to bring you up to the RDA.*
2 *Supplementation to take you beyond the RDA.*

You certainly must reach the RDA, by Stage 1 supplementation if necessary. As regards Stage 2, this book does its best to make an evaluation of all the current science.

The first vitamins and minerals listed below are those for which supplementation has the widest degree of support among the medical profession, generally speaking. That doesn't necessarily mean that the ones at the head of the list are the most important, only that they're the least controversial.

> **Insight**
>
> In general, food supplements should be taken with meals because they need the presence of other nutrients to perform as they should. But always read the label for each supplement in case there is a specific reason to do otherwise. (The interaction of nutrients is one of the factors that makes research so difficult.)

VITAMIN B12

If there's a vitamin about which more or less all of the medical community is agreed upon, it's vitamin B12. The evidence that absorption of this critical vitamin declines with age is irrefutable. You may well be getting enough when you're young but you probably won't be when you're older. Most elderly people suffer to some degree from atrophic gastritis, which means their stomachs don't produce enough hydrochloric acid, pepsin and intrinsic factor to absorb vitamin B12 from food.

What does it do for me?
Without vitamin B12, nerve fibres deteriorate, causing loss of balance, loss of skin sensation and muscle weakness. The Oxford Project to Investigate Memory and Ageing (OPTIMA) found that supplementation with vitamin B12 after age 60, together with folic acid and vitamin B6 (see below) slowed brain shrinkage by 30 per cent on average and, in certain cases, by more than 50 per cent. Deficiency can also cause megaloblastic anaemia, the symptoms of which include loss of appetite, diarrhoea, tiredness and tingling/numbness in the hands and feet.

What's the optimum dose?
The crystalline form of B12 in tablets can be absorbed even though natural B12 can't. A daily supplement of 6 mcg may be sufficient

initially, but the older you get the more you'll need. Dr John Lindenbaum of the Columbia Presbyterian Medical Center in the US recommends from 500 to 1,000 mcg a day for older people. The RDA is 2.4 mcg a day. The American National Academy of Sciences does not give any Tolerable Upper Intake Level. The reason for the huge discrepancy is that only a small proportion of the B12 ever gets absorbed.

Any side effects?
None that are known.

> **Insight**
>
> If you are a vegan you *must* take supplementary B12 unless you eat very large quantities of yeast extract – no other vegan foods contain sufficient.

DHA/EPA

DHA (docosahexaenoic acid) and EPA (eicosapentanoic acid) are the forms of omega-3 fatty acids (see previous chapter) that are the most beneficial. If you eat oily fish two or three times a week you should be getting enough and will *not* need a supplement. However, there are serious concerns about the level of toxic metals (such as mercury) in fish, especially those at the top of the food chain, bottom feeders and shellfish. Flaxseed (linseed) oil is a non-fish alternative but it contains omega-3 in the form of ALA (alpha-linolenic acid). The body can convert ALA to DHA and EPA but it's a rather inefficient process. To complicate things further, because of that inefficiency, you end up with a less than ideal proportion of DHA/EPA relative to omega-6 fatty acids in your body. Non-fish eaters should use flaxseed oil (see *Omega-3 fatty acids* on page 26) plus supplements. One style of non-fish supplement is prepared from algae (especially *Crypthecodinium cohnii* and *Schizochytrium*). Alternatively, you could take oil from the plant *Echium plantagineum* which has an omega 3: omega 6 ratio of about 1.5:1. Echium oil contains stearidonic acid (SDA) but a study published by the American Society for Nutritional Sciences in 2004 showed that it was easily metabolized to the highly beneficial EPA. Subjects who took 15 g of echium oil daily for four weeks had significantly improved blood profiles. Of the two kinds of supplement, I personally favour the algae, both in terms of cost and efficacy.

What does it do for me?
DHA/EPA supplementation:

- *protects against heart disease*
- *reduces cardiac arrhythmias*
- *lowers blood pressure*
- *combats arteriosclerosis*
- *helps prevent rheumatoid arthritis*
- *corrects anxiety and depression caused by deficiency*
- *improves memory in the elderly*
- *might extend life by protecting the telomeres on the chromosomes (see Chapter 1)*
- *increases the speed of communication in the brain.*

What's the optimum dose?
A daily supplement containing (or creating) around 200 mg DHA/EPA would be the minimum for those eating fish occasionally, or using flaxseed oil as recommended in the previous chapter. If you don't have other significant sources, at least double that.

Any side effects?
None have been reported at normal doses.

VITAMIN D

I omitted vitamin D from the first edition of this book because it seemed that most people had enough from a combination of food and sunlight (vitamin D3 is made in the skin when the UV index is greater than 3). But figures from the USA National Health and Nutrition Examination Survey have convinced me otherwise. They found that 70 per cent of children were either vitamin D deficient or insufficient. And the older you get, the more you need. There are five forms, D1 to D5, of which the most important to humans seem to be D2 (ergocalciferol) and D3 (cholecalciferol).

What does it do for me?
Vitamin D:

- ▶ *promotes healthy bones*
- ▶ *helps prevent osteoporosis*
- ▶ *may protect against the common cold and flu (a study of Japanese schoolchildren found that taking 1,200 IU daily resulted in 42 per cent less flu)*
- ▶ *may protect against multiple sclerosis (which is less common in the tropics)*
- ▶ *may improve brain function in later life*
- ▶ *may help maintain a healthy weight*
- ▶ *can reduce asthma symptoms*
- ▶ *reduces the risk of rheumatoid arthritis in women*
- ▶ *protects against radiation and cancer.*

What's the optimum dose?
The U.S. Food and Nutrition Board at the Institute of Medicine of the National Academies puts the adequate intake at 5 mcg (200 IU) up to the age of 50, 10 mcg (400 IU) from 51 to 70, and 15 mcg (600 IU) from 71 onwards. Some nutritionists, however, are urging much higher levels of 25 mcg (1,000 IU) and even more for the elderly. The only good natural food source of vitamin D is oily fish, but as with DHA/EPA (see pages 58–59) that comes at the price of ingesting toxic metals. Some foods are fortified with vitamin D but, in general, processed foods are a bad idea (see previous chapter). Just 15 minutes of good sunlight twice a week on the face, hands, arms, or back (without sunscreen) is believed to produce enough. But in winter many people fail to get that. I would therefore suggest a daily supplement of 10 mcg (400 IU) in winter which, combined with other sources, should ensure a healthy amount.

Any side effects?
The Tolerable Upper Intake Level (UL) is 50 mcg (2,000 IU) but many scientists see no problem with even 250 mcg (10,000 IU).

CALCIUM

Calcium is one of the eight major minerals in the body, and is the most abundant. Almost all of it is in your bones and teeth but about 1 per cent is required by your muscles and nerves, for blood clotting and to help various enzymes. When I wrote the first edition of this book it seemed clear that, given the importance of calcium, anyone falling short of the RDA should take a supplement. In 2010, however, everything was thrown into confusion by researchers at the University of Auckland, the University of Aberdeen, and Dartmouth University in the US. They examined the results from 15 trials involving nearly 12,000 people, some 88 per cent of them women, who were taking calcium supplements of at least 500 mg a day and concluded that there was an increased risk of heart attack in the region of 20–30 per cent. No such association has been found when the calcium comes from food. Some scientists have questioned the validity of the findings because, paradoxically, the researchers found no increased risk of stroke or death, which seems illogical.

Furthermore, in none of the 15 trials had the calcium supplementation been accompanied by vitamin D or any other substance known to help fix calcium in the bones (rather than the arteries), as is considered good practice. Nevertheless, until further research clarifies the matter, it seems sensible *not* to use calcium supplementation as a prophylactic (that is, to prevent osteoporosis). But if you know you have osteoporosis ('brittle bones') what should you do? Hormone replacement is an alternative strategy but that, too, has its problems. The consensus seems to be that calcium supplementation is still valid, under medical supervision and with vitamin D (or some other 'fixer').

What does it do for me?
First and foremost, calcium will keep your skeleton young, especially if you're a woman. In one French study of more than 3,000 women aged over 80, those who were given a daily supplement of 1,200 mg

of calcium plus 800 IU of vitamin D3 (which aids calcium absorption) had 43 per cent fewer hip fractures and 32 per cent fewer wrist, arm and pelvis fractures than those who received a placebo.

But calcium can do more for you than that. Here's a list of some of calcium's uses and benefits. Calcium:

- *fights osteoporosis and keeps the skeleton young*
- *reduces high blood pressure*
- *fights some cancers**
- *reduces 'bad' LDL cholesterol.*

Note: *Some researchers have found an association between high calcium intake and prostate cancer. To be on the safe side, men should make sure their total calcium intake doesn't exceed the adequate intake (below).

What's the optimum dose?
Our Stone Age ancestors ate between 2 and 3 grams of calcium a day. That's around four times more than most people eat now. There is no US RDA for calcium but the amount considered adequate for health (the AI) is 1,200 mg a day for men and women aged 51 or over (as against 1,000 mg for younger adults). The reason the AI is higher for older people is that as we age, we absorb less of the calcium we eat.

How much do we actually get? One study has put the average at as low as 500 mg. Very few of us seem to eat, let alone surpass, the US AI. On the other hand, it isn't difficult to obtain enough calcium from food. Here are some of the best sources:

	Mg calcium per 100 g
Cheddar cheese	740
Sesame seeds	670
Tofu	510
Sardines (canned)	430
Dried figs	250
Almonds	240

Only if you can't reach an adequate level from food should you take a supplement. Your doctor might suggest 500 mg or possibly even 1,000 mg. It's vital you should take it together with vitamin D which aids absorption and regulates the movement of calcium between your bones and your blood. A boron supplement will also help fix the calcium in the bones (boron occurs naturally in fruits and vegetables).

Any side effects?
At one time it was thought that a high calcium intake could lead to kidney stones (because kidney stones are normally composed of calcium oxalate). However, a study at Harvard's School of Public Health turned that thinking on its head by showing that a high intake of calcium was associated with a *lower* risk of kidney stones, and other studies have confirmed that. It seems the problem is more to do with the oxalate (a substance found in many foods but in especially large quantities in spinach, beet greens and rhubarb). Other contributors to stone formation are a high protein diet, salt and insufficient fluids. Always take your supplement with meals, because it will then tie up any oxalate and prevent it forming crystals.

With regards the association with prostate cancer, men should consult a doctor before taking a supplement that would elevate total calcium above the RDA.

As to the increased risk of heart attack found in the study quoted above, there is a logical mechanism that could explain it. If the extra calcium isn't absorbed by the bones (this is where the vitamin D comes in) the surplus calcium in the blood stream can get deposited on the walls of the arteries and form a foundation for fatty plaques – it's when the deposits break off that heart attacks occur. That mechanism was confirmed by a study by Dr Philip Greenland and Dr Tamar Polonsky at Northwestern University (also published in 2010) which found that men and women with high coronary artery calcium (CAC) were at greater risk of heart attack.

VITAMIN E

Vitamin E occurs in the highest concentrations in vegetable oils, nuts, seeds and whole grains. If you don't eat those foods you'll find it difficult to reach the US RDA.

What does it do for me?
Vitamin E gets pretty wide approval in the medical community as an antioxidant that (in particular) fights arteriosclerosis – the hardening and clogging of arteries. Vitamin E:

▶ *fights arteriosclerosis and helps keep arteries clear*
▶ *may fight cancer*
▶ *reduces cardiovascular disease*
▶ *helps prevent cataracts*
▶ *improves blood circulation in the brain and fights Alzheimer's*
▶ *boosts immunity*
▶ *reduces the swelling, pain and stiffness associated with rheumatoid arthritis.*

What's the optimum dose?
The US RDA for adults for vitamin E is 22.5 IU (15 mg), which it's just possible to get from food. But the average intake in the USA is only 14 IU (9 mg) for men and 9 IU (6 mg) for women. And even if you do reach the RDA, many studies have concluded that's far from enough to get the vitamin's full benefits. Research by Howard N. Hodis at the University of Southern California School of Medicine found that 100 IU a day for two years reduced the narrowing of the arteries due to arteriosclerosis. And research at the University of Texas in Dallas showed that 800 IU of vitamin E a day for three months cut the LDL oxidation of cholesterol by 40 per cent – the minimum intake necessary to get an effect was found to be 400 IU. Mary Sano at Columbia University together with the Alzheimer's Disease Cooperative Study Group tested 2,000 IU of vitamin E on Alzheimer's victims and concluded it reduced the need to be admitted to a nursing home by 58 per cent (however, the Tolerable Upper Intake Level has been set at 1,500 IU). So how much should you take? As ever, the first thing to do is maximize

your intake of vitamins and minerals from food. Good sources of vitamin E are:

	Alpha-tocopherol* (mg)	Gamma-tocopherol* (mg)
Almonds (1 oz/25 g)	7.4	0.2
Avocado (1 fruit)	2.7	0.4
Peanuts (1 oz/25 g)	2.4	2.4
Canola oil (1 tbs)	2.4	3.8
Olive oil (1 tbs)	1.9	0.1
Soybean oil (1 tbs)	1.1	8.7

Note: *Alpha-tocopherol is the form of vitamin E that has anti-oxidant properties and the one we're interested in here. The role of the gamma-tocopherol form of vitamin E isn't entirely clear. But in one study, gamma-tocopherol was shown to be protective against prostate cancer when the subjects also had high levels of alpha-tocopherol and selenium (as revealed by toenail analysis).

As regards supplementation on top, the Linus Pauling Institute now recommends a supplement of 200 IU (134 mg) a day. I would be a little more cautious and opt for 100 IU (67 mg) a day.

Any side effects?
Large doses of vitamin E – above the Tolerable Upper Intake Level – could increase the risk of haemorrhage. And an analysis of 19 clinical trials found that taking 2,000 IU a day caused a small increased risk of death. Taking 400 IU daily has been shown to accelerate the eye condition known as retinitis pigmentosa. Balancing risks and rewards, the suggested 100 IU daily supplement seems about right.

SELENIUM

Selenium is one of the eight trace elements known to be essential for human health. It occurs naturally in grains, sunflower seeds, meat, fish and garlic but, because levels seem to be diminishing in the soil, only Brazil nuts from the selenium-rich Amazonian soil contain a significant dose.

What does it do for me?
Selenium is an extremely powerful antioxidant, which means it can mop-up the free radicals that do so much damage to cells. It:

▶ *boosts the immune system*
▶ *fights cancer*
▶ *fights heart disease*
▶ *fights viruses*
▶ *fights depression.*

What's the optimum dose?
The US RDA for selenium is 55 mg a day, but a Swedish study suggests most people only get around half this. What's more, blood levels fall with age – by age 75 they will only be about three-quarters what they were when you were young. Unless you eat Brazil nuts every day (about six ready shelled or two freshly shelled) then you need a supplement. Anti-ageing specialists suggest 100–200 mg a day. The US Tolerable Upper Intake Level is 400 mcg, so there's little argument over this one.

Any side effects?
Selenium is toxic at high doses – probably around 2,500 mg a day.

MAGNESIUM

Magnesium occurs in quite high amounts in seeds, nuts, whole grains and legumes (peas, beans, lentils, etc.). If you include these in your daily diet you won't be deficient. But if you don't eat them regularly, you'll need a supplement.

What does it do for me?
Magnesium seems to be directly related to ageing. Animals that are deficient become old prematurely. Magnesium:

- *fights free radicals*
- *fights heart disease*
- *keeps the blood mobile*
- *reduces blood pressure*
- *combats diabetes*
- *fights osteoporosis*
- *protects mitochondria (the power sources inside your cells).*

What's the optimum dose?
The American RDA for magnesium used to be 300 mg a day but has been increased to 420 mg for men aged 31 and over, and to 320 mg for women aged 31 and over. Unfortunately, in one American study, two-thirds of older people were getting little more than 200 mg a day. Unless you're eating seeds, nuts, whole grains and legumes regularly you'll fall into that category and will need a supplement. Around 200 mg a day would be about right – the Tolerable Upper Intake Level for a supplement is 350 mg, so you'll be well within that.

Any side effects?
Going over 600 mg to 700 mg may cause diarrhoea.

> **Warning:** If you have kidney or heart problems consult a doctor before taking magnesium supplements.

ZINC

If you're a vegetarian, a vegan or just don't eat much meat, you're certain to be deficient in zinc. In fact, the only food with an abundance of zinc is the oyster.

What does it do for me?
At birth your thymus gland – in your neck just under your thyroid gland – was relatively huge and played a vital role in your immune system. But now it's much smaller and will steadily wither away as you get older. This is why, many researchers believe, elderly people

are much more prone to die from certain illnesses than young people. The way to save your thymus is to eat more zinc. Zinc has lots of benefits. It:

- ▶ *rejuvenates the thymus gland, thus boosting the immune system*
- ▶ *increases production of thymulin, associated with the production of lymphocytes*
- ▶ *increases production of interleukin 1, which helps to boost production of t-cells*
- ▶ *increases production of gamma interferon, essential to immune functioning*
- ▶ *increases levels of blood albumin, associated with longevity*
- ▶ *fights free radicals*
- ▶ *boosts testosterone and sperm count*
- ▶ *speeds wound healing*
- ▶ *may play a role in helping prevent macular degeneration of the eyes.*

Insight

Zinc deficiency in men leads to lowered testosterone and, in extreme cases, impotence. If you are having a problem then a zinc supplement is one of the things you should try.

What's the optimum dose?

The US RDA for zinc is 11 mg a day for men and 8 mg for women. One study suggests the typical Western diet only just reaches this level. What's more, many anti-ageing specialists believe that between 15 mg and 30 mg a day is the optimum dose. The Tolerable Upper Intake Level is 40 mg, so you'll be perfectly safe if you take 15 mg as a supplement.

Any side effects?

No side effects have been observed at 50 mg a day.

CHROMIUM

It's difficult to get sufficient quantities of this trace element from food.

What does it do for me?
Chromium helps regulate insulin. Without sufficient chromium you
risk insulin and sugar damage to your arteries – creating plaque –
as well as diabetes. Essentially, chromium enhances the effect of
insulin, so you need less of it. That in turn reduces the risk of
developing insulin resistance. Chromium:

▶ *reduces insulin damage to arteries*
▶ *normalizes blood sugar*
▶ *combats diabetes*
▶ *lowers bad LDL cholesterol*
▶ *increases good HDL cholesterol*
▶ *boosts the immune system*
▶ *combats heart disease*
▶ *boosts the hormone DHEA which falls dramatically with age.*

What's the optimum dose?
The American authorities used to say that 200 mcg of chromium
a day was necessary for health. But the new Adequate Intake
given by the American National Academy of Sciences is only
30–35 mcg a day for men, and 20–25 mcg for women. The AI,
remember, is the intake observed in healthy people and 'assumed
to be adequate'. But 90 per cent of American men are estimated to
have less than the AI. And, in fact, pro-chromium scientists believe
the old level of 200 mcg a day is, in fact, the minimum for healthy
people, rising to between 400 and 1,000 mcg if you have diabetes
or high cholesterol. No Tolerable Upper Intake Level has been
set due to a lack of data but some experts believe you could take
several thousand mcg a day without problems. A supplement of
200 mcg is considered perfectly safe.

Warning: If you are injecting insulin for diabetes, don't begin a
chromium supplement without consulting your doctor because
your insulin requirement may change.

Any side effects?
None are known at the suggested levels.

FOLIC ACID (ALSO KNOWN AS FOLATE AND FOLACIN)

Most people probably know folic acid or folate as the B group vitamin that's recommended for pregnant women. In fact, everybody needs it.

What does it do for me?
Folic acid's most dramatic property is its ability to lower homocysteine, a significant risk factor for blocked arteries and heart disease. But it does plenty more; it:

- *fights heart disease*
- *protects arteries*
- *preserves mental function*
- *improves mood and combats depression*
- *fights cancer: especially of the cervix, lung, oesophagus, breast and colon.*

What's the optimum dose?
The US RDA for folic acid is 400 mcg a day (600 mcg for pregnant women). Various studies suggest the typical Western diet provides only half that, so a supplement is essential. Smokers need more than non-smokers. Dr Linus Pauling recommended 400–800 mcg a day and some experts go as far as 1,000–8,000 mcg a day. However, given the possible side effects (see below) a supplement of 200 mcg seems to be a safe and suitable level for most people. If bread were to be fortified with folic acid, as some have proposed, no further supplement should be taken.

Any side effects?
Folic acid supplements used to be discouraged on the grounds they could mask the symptoms of pernicious anaemia. However, with new diagnostic methods, that no longer applies. More significant is new research from the Institute of Food Research which suggests that high doses can lead to unmetabolized folic acid in the blood stream. That in turn could increase the risk of bowel cancer in those with a family history as well as causing problems for those being treated for arthritis and leukaemia.

BETA-CAROTENE

Beta-carotene is probably the easiest vitamin to remember because it's found in the largest quantities in carrots.

What does it do for me?
Beta-carotene is a powerful antioxidant, protecting the genes in your cells from free radical damage. It:

▶ *helps vision (especially in dim light)*
▶ *promotes healthy skin*
▶ *promotes normal bone development.*
▶ *fights cancer*
▶ *combats heart attacks and strokes.*

What's the optimum dose?
Various studies have used daily supplements of between 10 and 50 mg with highly beneficial effects.

Top tip

> Beta-carotene, which is found in many plant foods, especially carrots, sweet potatoes and apricots, can convert to retinol (vitamin A) in the body. However, beta-carotene and vitamin A are not the same thing. To get the benefits of beta-carotene, make sure that any supplement you take is beta-carotene and not retinol-type vitamin A.

Any side effects?
At least two studies have concluded that beta-carotene increases the risk of lung cancer in smokers. Others suggest beta-carotene increases the risk of heart attacks in those who have already had a heart attack. These are puzzling findings that are at variance with a great deal of other research.

VITAMIN C

Vitamin C is one of the most famous vitamins and rightly so.
It's involved in an enormous number of bodily processes.

What does it do for me?

Vitamin C is essential for the synthesis of collagen, without which
your body would simply fall apart. Researchers have shown that it
protects against getting cancer, boosts the immune system, reduces
gum disease, and protects arteries, lungs and even sperm. Various
studies indicate that increasing vitamin C intake:

- *leads to the manufacture of more antibody molecules*
- *boosts the lymphocyte defence against cancer*
- *reduces the severity of cold and flu symptoms*
- *speeds wound healing and increases the strength of scar tissue*
- *helps increase muscle strength*
- *helps reduce high cholesterol*
- *destroys some toxins in the body*
- *raises IQ levels (in those who are deficient in vitamin C)*
- *reduces allergic reactions*
- *eases symptoms of asthma*
- *helps prevent cataracts*
- *helps control glaucoma*
- *helps prevent and control gingivitis.*

What's the optimum dose?

The US RDA is 90 mg a day for men, and 75 mg a day for
women (rising to 120 mg if breast feeding). In reality, a quarter of
Americans get less than 60 mg a day. And in one study, as many
as 68 per cent of elderly patients were found to have white blood
cells deficient in vitamin C. So supplementation is indicated for
some groups, even according to mainstream medical opinion.
The question is, how far should you go?

If you're not ill, a reasonable amount would be 1,000 mg a day,
taken as two doses so as to maintain a consistent level. This is the

minimum that was advised by Linus Pauling and is well within the Tolerable Upper Intake Level of 2,000 mg given by America's National Academy of Sciences. However, the Linus Pauling Institute now suggests two daily doses of 250 mg, making a total of 500 mg, which you may feel is more prudent.

When you feel a cold coming on, however, the situation is different. Irwin Stone, who wrote a book called *The Healing Factor: Vitamin C Against Disease*, recommended 1,500–2,000 mg of vitamin C at the first sign of a cold, repeated every half-hour. According to him, only three doses were usually necessary. Some doctors scorned his claims, others replicated his findings.

A study carried out in 1977 settled the issue of vitamin C and colds for many. Some subjects began a course of 6,000 mg of vitamin C a day on the first day of a cold, some on the second and some on the third. A fourth group was given a placebo. Those treated on the first day did the best. Their colds lasted an average of 3.6 days and only 13 per cent had complications. Those who started treatment on the third day were ill for an average of nine days and 41 per cent had complications – similar to the placebo group. So, for vitamin C to be fully effective, both correct dose and timing are required.

Vitamin C and cancer

There have been conflicting studies on the impact of vitamin C supplementation on those who *already* have cancer. Arthur Robinson was President and Research Director of the Linus Pauling Institute when Linus Pauling was still alive. The two men fell out when Arthur Robinson's experiments showed that giving mice with squamous cell carcinoma doses of vitamin C equivalent to between 1 g and 5 g in humans *accelerated* the growth of the tumours.

In simple terms the explanation seems to be this. Vitamin C is good for normal cells but it's even better for certain types of cancer cell, enabling them to proliferate more rapidly – twice as fast in the case of Mr Robinson's experiment. (In the same way, many other things that are good for the body are also good for cancer cells, so it's not just a case of vitamin C.) One mechanism by which it's agreed vitamin C *can* kill cancer cells is when the dose is so high it actually becomes toxic, the cancer cells being more vulnerable than normal cells. But no one is suggesting self-medication at that level.

At the moment the picture remains confused. Some studies report that vitamin C in large but not toxic doses suppresses cancer (especially in conjunction with other vitamins and minerals) while others report no effect or a harmful effect. There's also controversy about the interaction with conventional cancer therapies. But what seems certain is that if you *don't* have cancer, then vitamin C at the recommended dose will produce numerous health benefits.

Insight

In Mr Robinson's experiments, tumours on the 'vitamin C mice' grew twice as fast as on the normal mice, but those on calorie-restricted (CR) mice grew at only a tenth of the speed for normal mice – an amazing twentyfold difference between the two extremes. To learn more about CR see pages 35–38.

Any (other) side effects?

Very large doses can cause diarrhoea. Some scientists think that high doses of vitamin C increase the risk of kidney stones, although others disagree. A study led by Professor James Dwyer of the University of Southern California Medical School found that vitamin C caused thickening of the walls of the arteries. This was interpreted as harmful plaque build-up. However, other scientists came to the completely different conclusion that the thickening was a beneficial strengthening of the arteries and not plaque at all.

VITAMIN B6

Whole grains, nuts, soya, bananas, sweet potatoes and seafood are all high in vitamin B6 and will just about take you to the RDA but there's evidence that more is better.

What does it do for me?
Vitamin B6 works together with folic acid to combat homocysteine and thus lower the risk of arteriosclerosis. But that's not all. It:

▶ *protects blood vessels*
▶ *helps long-term memory*
▶ *boosts the immune system*
▶ *shrinks the synovial membranes that line the joints, thus improving mobility*
▶ *reduces symptoms of carpal tunnel syndrome.*

What's the optimum dose?
The US RDA for vitamin B6 is 1.7 mg a day for men aged 51 and over, and 1.5 mg a day for women aged 51 and over. The typical Western diet just about reaches these levels. But researchers at Tufts University improved the immune function in older people with slightly higher doses of 2.88 mg for men and 1.9 mg for women. And to reduce homocysteine, 10–50 mg a day seems to be necessary. The Tolerable Upper Intake Level is 100 mg a day so a supplement of not more than 50 mg seems to be both safe and beneficial.

Any side effects?
Very high doses, of the order of 2,000 mg a day, may cause neurological damage in some people, but that's 40 times the dose suggested above.

RESVERATROL

Resveratrol is a chemical produced by certain plants, especially vines and the Japanese knotweed, in response to attack by bacteria and fungi. The beneficial effects of drinking red wine (see page 29) are often attributed to resveratrol but the concentration in red wine is quite low. A supplement is a far more powerful alternative and without the risks posed by alcohol.

What does it do for me?

Most research so far has been on animals with very little on humans. But from what we know so far, resveratrol:

- *may activate a 'survival gene' known as SIRT-1*
- *may protect telomeres, the 'caps' on the ends of chromosomes, the shortening of which is thought by some scientists to be a key factor in ageing*
- *is a potent anti-cancer agent, according to a 2010 study*
- *arrests the growth of human squamous cell carcinoma, according to the same 2010 study*
- *may protect against cardiovascular disease*
- *protects against Alzheimer's disease*
- *is an antioxidant*
- *is an anti-inflammatory*
- *significantly increases testosterone.*

What's the optimum dose?

At the time of writing, GlaxoSmithKline is still working on a pharmaceutical-grade version of resveratrol, but you can buy lower-potency food supplements now. The effective dose in humans is unknown, but these supplements are generally in the range of 50 mg–250 mg of resveratrol.

Any side effects?

Resveratrol is not known to have any adverse effects on humans but no long-term trials have been carried out. Doses up to 300 mg per kilo of bodyweight given over four weeks (22.5 grams for a person weighing 75 kg) caused no problems – that's around 200 times the kind of dose you'll get in a supplement.

Combining vitamin and mineral supplements

We already know that vitamins and minerals in food work better than those taken as supplements. The effect of any one nutrient seems to be boosted by the presence of others. So, following the same principle, it would seem to make sense to take several supplements together and at the same time as food. For example:

▶ *America's National Institute on Ageing found that vitamin C and E supplements together halved the death rate among those aged 67 to 105.*
▶ *The National Cancer Institute in China concluded that supplements of beta carotene, vitamin E and selenium reduced cancer deaths by 13 per cent.*
▶ *In a study by Dr Donald Lamm at West Virginia University, high doses of vitamins A, B6, C and E plus zinc slashed the appearance of new tumours in cancer patients by half.*

Insight

Does a multivitamin make good sense? You're probably better to design your own multivitamin and mineral package by combining individual substances. That way, you can be sure of getting the optimum quantity of each one. The B group vitamins are an exception. One tablet is usually fine for all of them.

10 THINGS TO REMEMBER

1 *Orthomolecular medicine is the maintenance of health and the treatment of disease using substances naturally present in the body, but as doses from 50 to 300 times the RDA – and, in some circumstances, even more.*

2 *RDA stands for Recommended Daily Amount (UK) or Recommended Dietary Allowance (USA) – the quantity of a nutrient that is officially considered to be adequate for health.*

3 *The medical establishment isn't, in general, persuaded by the case for supplementary vitamins and minerals, but many scientists and doctors are convinced of their effectiveness, especially for older people who can't easily obtain even the RDA for all vitamins from food alone.*

4 *DHA/EPA deficiency is common because oily fish and flaxseed oil are the only natural sources.*

5 *Deficiencies of vitamins B12, D and E are common, especially in the elderly; beta-carotene, B6 and C are not usually deficient but more, up to a point, is better.*

6 *Calcium supplementation can combat osteoporosis, but in the light of recent concerns it should only be taken together with vitamin D and under medical supervision.*

7 *Deficiencies of the minerals selenium, magnesium, zinc and chromium are common.*

8 *Folic acid protects the heart and arteries.*

9 *Resveratrol may activate a 'survival' gene for longer life.*

10 *Combining vitamins and minerals can magnify the beneficial effects.*

HOW MUCH LONGER ARE YOU GOING TO LIVE NOW?

▶ *Are you aware of the micronutrients essential for good health?*

▶ *Are you monitoring your diet for possible deficiencies?*

▶ *If you're an older person or vegan, are you taking supplementary vitamin B12?*

▶ *Unless you eat oily fish regularly (not recommended) do you use flaxseed oil and take supplementary DHA/EPA?*

▶ *If you're not often out of doors in the sunshine (but not too much) do you take a vitamin D supplement?*

▶ *Have you (if middle-aged or more) been checked for osteoporosis, and if positive, have you discussed calcium supplementation with your doctor?*

▶ *Are you making sure you have the optimum doses for vitamins E, folic acid, beta-carotene, C and B6?*

▶ *Are you making sure you have the optimum doses for the minerals selenium, magnesium, zinc and chromium?*

▶ *Are you taking resveratrol?*

▶ *If using supplements, are you taking them with food/as directed on the packet?*

Score:

If you answered 'yes' to six or more questions you're obviously very serious about living longer and are taking the steps that will be rewarded by a significant increase in your life expectancy. Move on to the next chapter.

If you answered 'yes' to between three and five questions you're well on the way to a better lifestyle. You can also move on to the next chapter but re-read this one from time to time and keep monitoring your intake of micronutrients.

If you answered 'yes' to two or fewer questions you undoubtedly want to live longer (who doesn't?) but you're leaving things to chance (which may or may not work out well). Give thought to taking more charge of your nutrient intake. Move on to the next chapter but revisit this one in a few weeks' time when you've had the opportunity to mull everything over.

4

....

Exercise

In this chapter you will learn:
- *how exercise can extend your life*
- *how exercise can improve the quality of your life*
- *how exercise can make you look younger*
- *how exercise can make you feel happier.*

Early in 2007 three muggers pushed Buster Martin up against a wall and tried to steal his money. Using some karate he'd learned he, in his own words, 'just kicked out and my feet homed in on the right place.' A little later in the year Buster's band, The Zimmers, enjoyed enormous success with a cover of 'My Generation'. So a pretty eventful few months for anybody, but especially for Buster because he was then 100.

Naturally, everybody wanted to know the secret of not just a long but also an active life. When *The Times* interviewed him, he particularly mentioned work (three days a week as a mechanic and car valet at a plumbing company), diet (good red meat, vegetables and eggs but not fish or dairy products) and exercise. Buster was still doing 16-km (10-mile) runs.

Noel Johnson took up running at the age of 70, completed his first marathon two years later, recorded his best marathon time at age 84 and celebrated his 92nd birthday by running the New York Marathon. He wrote a book about it all called *A Dud At 70; A Stud At 80.*

And it's not just men who do these 'crazy' things. Ruth Rothfarb started running when she was 72. At age 92 she had this to say: 'When I started running 20 years ago people said I was an old lady and that I'd drop dead doing it. But most of *them* dropped dead and I'm still running around.' At that time she was still covering 16–24 km (10–15 miles) a day. One much younger runner who danced with her at a post-marathon party when she was in her eighties testified that she could 'really swing'.

When he was in his mid-fifties, Norton Davey was 'a coronary waiting to happen'. His doctor advised exercise. Norton began walking, then jogging and then added swimming and cycling. At age 82 he became the oldest person to complete an Ironman Triathlon – 4 km (2.4 miles) of swimming, a 180-km (112-mile) bike ride and a 42-km (26.2-mile) marathon.

All of which illustrates two things. Exercise not only helps you live longer but, just as important, it improves the quality of your later years as well.

None of this is new, of course. Over 2,000 years ago Hippocrates observed that: 'All parts of the body which have a function, if used in moderation and exercised in labours to which each is accustomed, become thereby healthy and well developed, and age slowly; but if unused and left idle, they become liable to disease, defective in growth, and age quickly.' A doctor today probably wouldn't put it very differently.

So why is it that so many of us exercise so little? Of course, in Hippocrates' time it was hard not to get enough exercise, unless you were wealthy enough to have a chariot and slaves to get it ready for you. Nowadays most of us have to make a special effort to get fit. But we have one advantage. Exercise may not be unavoidable but it is fun. Yes, *fun*. If you didn't know that, then let me tell you you've been missing out on something great.

··

Insight

Okay, so maybe it's sometimes a little bit painful to start with but once you've acclimatized, exercise can give you a pretty .

big rush. Within a few weeks you'll be looking at your watch counting the hours and minutes to your next session, your next 'fix'. I promise you. And there are so many different ways of exercising that it's hard to label them all 'boring' or 'not for me'. How about volleyball on the beach, for example? Why not a miniature trampoline in the back garden? What about jogging around the park with a group of friends? There are literally hundreds of different exercise activities.

Up to ten more years

Let's cut to the bottom line. How much do you have to exercise and how many years can you gain? Any exercise is good and more is better. But if you want to put a figure to it, a study led by Oscar Franco at the Erasmus M.C. University Medical Center concluded that walking 30 minutes a day, five days a week extended life by around 18 months compared with being a couch potato, while running the same amount of time extended life by almost four years. Men seem to benefit even more than women. A study of nearly half a million men aged 45 to 90 by E. C. Hammond in 1964 showed conclusively that death rates fell significantly as exercise levels increased. Those following a 'heavy' exercise regime increased their life expectancy by more than ten years compared with those who took no exercise. So the motto is: Don't sit if you can walk, don't walk if you can run.

And it's not just a matter of extra years. It's also to do with quality of life. If you keep fit you'll be able to enjoy activities your sedentary peers have had to give up. You'll look better. You'll have stronger bones, improved muscle tone and a leaner profile. You'll have better brain function and more self-confidence. And you'll have fewer health problems because your immune system will be stronger.

Here are some of the things that happen to our bodies as we age:

▶ *The heart's ability to pump oxygen declines 1 per cent a year after maturity.*

- *Muscle power declines 1 per cent a year after age 50.*
- *The number of muscle fibres declines 3–5 per cent a decade after age 30.*
- *Because the chest wall stiffens, the amount of oxygen available to the body drops 50 per cent for men and 29 per cent for women by age 75.*
- *The speed of nerve messages drops 10–15 per cent by age 70.*
- *Bone loss averages 15–20 per cent in men and 25–30 per cent in women by age 70.*
- *Flexibility declines 20–30 per cent by age 70; the range of motion in the knee declines 33 per cent and in the hip 38 per cent between the ages of 35 and 90.*

And here are some of the things exercise can do to combat that. You will:

- *increase your life expectancy by two to four years*
- *feel happier*
- *sleep better*
- *have more energy*
- *look better*
- *enjoy greater self-esteem*
- *think more clearly*
- *handle stress more easily*
- *have a reduced risk of heart attack*
- *increase your levels of HDL or 'good' cholesterol*
- *lower your blood pressure*
- *increase your bone density*
- *boost your immune system*
- *enhance your sexual responsiveness.*

Insight

Your heart beats, perhaps, 70–80 times a minute when you're not exerting yourself, which works out at something like 37 million times a year. Now consider what would happen if you could lower your resting heart rate by ten beats a minute – which you easily could through exercise. Even though you might add half a million extra beats a year during the exercise, the overall saving would be something like six million beats a year. That means you'd save a whole year's worth of heartbeats every six years.

How exercise makes you feel happier

How happy would you say you are? I hope you're answering: 'Very happy'. It is normally the case that as we get older we get happier. We're more skilful at it and we have a better perspective. But that doesn't apply to everybody.

There's a special kind of depression, ranging from mild to severe, that comes on in middle age, called involutional melancholia. It's not a very flattering title. The dictionary defines involution as 'degeneration' and 'structural deformation'. In other words, it's low feelings associated with a decline in bodily efficiency. It could be purely physical. It could be psychological. It could be a combination.

As we've just seen, you can slow that decline through exercise. But there's far more to it than that. Exercise positively encourages happiness by boosting the body's production of what you might call 'happy chemicals', described below.

ENDORPHINS

The word means 'endogenous morphine', that's to say, morphine-like substances produced by the body. Endorphins combat pain, promote happiness and are one of the ingredients in the exercise euphoria known as the 'runner's high'. Twelve minutes of exercise is all it takes to increase endorphins by 500 per cent.

PHENYLETHYLAMINE (PEA)

PEA is a powerful mood booster, as proven by researchers at Rush University and the Center for Creative Development, Chicago.

Meanwhile, scientists at Nottingham Trent University in the UK discovered that PEA levels increase significantly following exercise. There are other ways of augmenting PEA. You could fall in love – it's exactly the same chemical that produces the 'walking on air' feeling. It's also present in chocolate as well as some fizzy drinks, but it seems very little is absorbed. So exercise seems the most reliable PEA booster. The researchers at Nottingham Trent University found that running at 70 per cent of maximum heart rate (MHR) for 30 minutes increased the level of phenylacetic acid in the urine (which reflects phenylethylamine) by 77 per cent.

NORADRENALINE/NOREPINEPHRINE (NE)

When generated by exercise (as opposed to stress), noradrenaline tends to make you feel happy, confident, positive and expansive. Eight minutes of vigorous exercise will boost it ten times.

SEROTONIN

The link with exercise isn't so strong for this one but serotonin is a neurotransmitter for happiness and there's reason to think exercise elevates its level in the brain.

OTHER HAPPY EFFECTS

In addition to increasing 'happy chemicals', exercise *lowers* the level of cortisol, a stress hormone linked with low mood.

There are also two further processes at work:

- ▶ **Thermogenics:** *Exercise increases the body's core temperature, which in turn relaxes muscles which in turn induces a feeling of tranquillity.*
- ▶ **Right brain/left brain:** *Repetitive physical activities such as jogging 'shut down' the left side of the brain (logical thought) freeing up the right brain (creative thought). It's a kind of meditation and it's why solutions to*

seemingly intractable problems often appear 'by magic'
when exercising.

EXERCISE AND DEPRESSION

Exercise is so good at improving mood that it's actually become a
standard treatment for depression, as recommended in the UK by
the National Institute for Health and Clinical Excellence (NICE).
In carefully controlled trials, exercise has performed just as well
as antidepressants in combating depression, but without the side
effects of drugs.

When you think about it, it's not hard to understand how human
beings evolved that way. Our ancestors had to be capable of
vigorous activity if they were to eat. When their muscles screamed
for respite, those whose bodies produced chemicals to ease the pain
were the ones who ran down the prey and got the food. Logically,
they were also the ones evolution selected. Well, that's a simplistic
way of putting it but right in essence. Nowadays we only have to be
capable of lifting a can off a shelf but our bodies remain unchanged.
So if you want to enjoy those same chemicals, get some exercise.

How fit are you?

In Britain, about four-fifths of people don't get enough exercise.
That's an awful lot of less-than-optimum lifespans. Join the
one-fifth who do!

You need to:

▶ *exercise for fitness*
▶ *exercise for strength*
▶ *exercise for flexibility.*

Let's see how you're doing at the moment. Make a note of the
letter, a–f, that corresponds with your answer.

1 What's your resting heart rate (that is, your pulse when you wake up in the morning)? *(See page 92.)*

    a *Under 50*
    b *50–60*
    c *61–70*
    d *71–80*
    e *81–90*
    f *Over 90*

2 Can you touch the floor with your legs straight? *(Warm up a little before trying this.)*

    a *I can touch the floor with the palms of my hands.*
    b *I can touch the floor with the tips of my fingers.*
    c *I can touch my ankle bones.*
    d *I can't get further than my calves.*

3 How many sit-ups can you do in one minute?
(**Don't do this if you have a back problem.** *To do sit-ups, lie on your back on the carpet, knees bent, heels about 46 cm/18 inches from your buttocks, feet flat on the floor shoulder-width apart and anchored under a heavy piece of furniture. Your hands should be on the sides of your head. When reclining you only need to touch your shoulders to the floor.)*

    a *More than 50*
    b *40–50*
    c *30–39*
    d *20–29*
    e *10–19*

4 How long does it take you to walk 0.8 km (0.5 mile)? *(Measure the distance along a flat stretch of road/pavement using your car.)*

    a *Under 6 minutes*
    b *6–7 minutes*

c *7–8 minutes*
d *8–9 minutes*
e *9–10 minutes*
f *Over 10 minutes*

Your score
Add up your score, using the tables below.

Question 1

	Men	Women
a	23	25
b	18	20
c	13	15
d	8	10
e	3	5
f	0	0

Question 2

	Men (age)			Women (age)		
	40–49	50–59	Over 60	40–49	50–59	Over 60
a	20	23	25	20	22	23
b	10	15	20	8	13	18
c	5	10	15	3	8	13
d	0	5	10	0	4	8

Question 3

	Men (age)			Women (age)		
	40–49	50–59	Over 60	40–49	50–59	Over 60
a	25	-	-	-	-	-
b	20	25	-	25	-	-
c	15	20	25	20	25	-
d	10	15	20	15	20	25
e	5	10	15	10	15	20

Question 4

	Men (age)			Women (age)		
	40–49	50–59	Over 60	40–49	50–59	Over 60
a	20	25	-	25	-	-
b	15	20	25	20	25	-
c	10	15	20	15	20	25
d	5	10	15	10	15	20
e	1	5	10	5	10	15
f	0	1	5	1	5	10

If you scored 75–100 you're already extremely fit, strong and flexible – keep it up and you'll stay on course for those extra years of well-being.

If you scored 50–74 you're not in bad shape, but if you do a little more you'll gain benefits in terms of longevity and health.

If you scored under 50 then, in one way, you're lucky because you're going to improve rapidly once you start exercising regularly – you'll notice a difference very quickly.

Exercising for fitness

If you don't take any exercise at all at the moment the whole idea may seem rather daunting. But look at it this way, as a complete beginner you're going to improve very quickly. You'll be amazed at how rapidly you'll progress.

Good exercises for fitness include:

▶ *jogging*
▶ *cycling*
▶ *swimming*.

But before we take a look at them let's take a look at exactly what you need to achieve.

Target number 1: Exercise at your optimum 'training heart rate'
Your optimum training heart rate (THR) is the level at which you'll get the maximum benefit for the minimum discomfort.

The first requirement is to know your maximum heart rate (MHR) – the level at which your heart just can't beat any faster. It can be worked out in a fitness laboratory but there is an easier and less exhausting (although less precise) way. To calculate your MHR use the following formula: 220 – your age.

For example, if you're 50 years old your MHR will be: 220 – 50 = 170.

The next step is to relate that to your THR. Experts argue about the percentage of MHR that provides the best training heart rate (THR). But most people are agreed that as a minimum, THR should be at least 60 per cent of MHR. Beyond 70 per cent of MHR, exercise would be classed as 'vigorous'. At 70 to 80 per cent you'd be in the zone where aerobic conditioning improves the most. You wouldn't want to go beyond 80 per cent, unless you were seriously training to win races. So let's stick with the assumption that you're 50 years old and intending to exercise at the 70 per cent level. The calculation would look like this:

$(220 - 50) \times 70$ per cent $= 170 \times 70$ per cent $= 119$

At that level you should be able to carry on a conversation – with a little bit of puffing.

Target number 2: lower your resting heart rate
Your resting heart rate (RHR) is the level when you wake up in the morning and before you get out of bed. It's the measure of how well your exercise programme is going. The average RHR for men

is 60 to 80 beats per minute, while for women it's somewhat higher at 70 to 90 beats a minute.

If you're at 100 beats or more you're clearly not getting sufficient exercise. You should be aiming to get under 60. Athletes tend to be in the 40 to 50 range. RHRs under 30 have been known.

If you have a fairly high RHR you should be able to reduce it by one beat per minute per week during the first ten weeks of an exercise programme (such as the one given on pages 94–95). You'll be able to see quick results and that's very good for motivation.

Taking your pulse

The easiest place to take your pulse is to one side of your Adam's apple. Just press gently with three fingers and you'll feel it. Another place is on your wrist. Turn your hand palm upwards and place four fingers of your other hand lengthwise with your little finger at the base of your thumb. You should feel the pulse either under your forefinger or middle finger. Count for 15 seconds and multiply by four.

However, it's not very easy taking your pulse accurately while you're exercising. A better idea is to buy a heart rate monitor with a watch-style display on your wrist. They're available quite cheaply in sports equipment shops.

Warning: The NHS warns that if you haven't been exercising regularly and have any of the following characteristics you should check with your doctor before beginning an exercise programme.

▶ *Over 35 and a smoker*
▶ *Over 40 and inactive*
▶ *Diabetic*
▶ *At risk of heart disease*

> ▸ *High blood pressure*
> ▸ *High cholesterol*
> ▸ *Experience chest pains while exercising*
> ▸ *Difficulty breathing during mild exertion.*

Do what you enjoy

The best fitness exercise is something you enjoy and will be happy to do several times a week. It's no good relying on, say, a ski trip once a year or a game of tennis once a month. So when you're choosing, bear in mind practical considerations such as cost, distance from your home and the availability of friends (if it's something you can't do on your own).

JOGGING

Jogging is a lot of fun because the steady, rhythmical movement seems to generate more 'happy' chemicals per minute than many other activities.

Advantages

▸ *Doesn't require any special equipment, apart from a good pair of running shoes.*
▸ *Doesn't have to cost anything.*
▸ *Doesn't require any special training.*
▸ *Provides plenty of fresh air and sunshine out of doors.*
▸ *Can be done indoors on a machine when the weather is bad.*
▸ *Can be done alone or with friends.*
▸ *Can be done anywhere.*
▸ *Enhances creative thinking and permits 'meditation'.*
▸ *Makes progress very easy to measure.*
▸ *The impact is good for bone density in the legs.*

Disadvantages

▸ *Can be hard on the joints.*
▸ *Not much exercise for the upper body.*

One of the problems is running slowly enough. Yes, *slowly*. Beginners tend to associate the word running with 'going fast'. Wrong. Don't rush. You're aiming for a pace you can sustain over a long period. That means going a lot slower than your sprinting pace. In fact, to begin with you should try to run no quicker than the pace of a brisk walk. It's not as easy as you might think to go that slowly. If you can hardly speak you're going too fast.

Here's a little programme to help you build up from zero to a reasonable level of happy-fitness in just ten weeks. At the end of it you can just continue at the week ten level on three to five days or, if you really get inspired, you might like to run further.

Your ten-week jogging programme
If you can jog along *slowly* for a minute at a time, then you can begin the programme (but see the Warning on page 92).
If you can't – and that goes for lots of people – then you'll need to follow a pre-programme. Just begin by walking. Maybe get off the bus a stop early and stroll the rest of the way. Walk down a flight of stairs rather than take the lift. Later, walk up a flight of stairs. Gradually walk more and more vigorously. Swing your arms. Now and then put in half a dozen jogging strides; then a dozen; then 20.

Once you're ready for the ten-week programme, think in terms of keeping moving briskly for about 20 minutes *plus* 5 minutes warming up and 5 minutes cooling down, making a total of 30 minutes in all. Exercise at least three times a week and build up to five times. Don't run too fast – at all times you should be able to carry on a conversation.

Week 1   Alternate 1 minute of running with 2 minutes of walking
Week 2   Alternate 2 minutes of running with 2 minutes of walking

Week 3   Alternate 3 minutes of running with 2 minutes of walking
Week 4   Alternate 5 minutes of running with 2 minutes of walking
Week 5   Alternate 6 minutes of running with 1.5 minutes of walking
Week 6   Alternate 8 minutes of running with 1.5 minutes of walking
Week 7   Run 10 minutes, walk 1.5 minutes, run 10 minutes
Week 8   Run 12 minutes, walk 1 minute, run 8 minutes
Week 9   Run 15 minutes, walk 1 minute, run 5 minutes
Week 10 Run 20 minutes.

Insight

When I was heading towards my fiftieth birthday a friend challenged me to run a marathon. I hadn't run since school days and when I had my first practice I couldn't run for 42 seconds without getting out of breath, let alone 42 km (26 miles). But with nine months of training I completed my first marathon, and in a respectable time. So I know it can be done.

CYCLING

Like running, cycling can be done indoors or outdoors.

Advantages

▶ *One of the best forms of exercise.*
▶ *Easy on the joints.*
▶ *Provides plenty of fresh air and sunshine out of doors.*
▶ *Can be done indoors on a machine when the weather is bad.*
▶ *Can be done alone or with friends.*
▶ *Makes progress very easy to measure.*

Disadvantages

▶ *You need a bicycle.*
▶ *Not much exercise for the upper body.*
▶ *If you ride on the road there's an element of danger.*

SWIMMING

Swimming is just about the only form of exercise you'll relish when the weather is hot. It's also extremely easy on the joints. On the other hand, the total lack of impact means it does little to increase bone density – an important consideration as you get older.

Advantages

- ▶ *You can easily keep doing it in hot weather.*
- ▶ *Easy on the joints.*
- ▶ *Good for upper body strength.*

Disadvantages

- ▶ *Unless you have your own, you have to make the effort to go to a swimming pool.*
- ▶ *Many swimming pools are too crowded for serious exercise.*
- ▶ *Does nothing to increase bone density.*

Insight

Lots of people nowadays are talking about 'wild swimming'. Fortunately, where I live it's possible, and it certainly introduces a whole new dimension. If you don't care for swimming pools, see if you can find a wild swimming spot near you and enjoy nature as you get fit.

Exercising for strength

You've probably not thought about exercising for *strength*. It possibly even sounds fanatical and, if you're a woman, unfeminine. Well, I'm going to try to convince you otherwise.

As we've seen, you start losing muscle fibres from around the age of 30 and muscle power tends to decline about 1 per cent a year after the age of 50. That may not sound a lot but by age 70 it's getting serious. Having to rely on other people for everyday tasks like opening a jar isn't the way you want to be. What's more, it's muscles that give bodies their masculine *and* feminine contours. Breasts are, to some extent, held up by muscles. Buttocks *are* muscles. Legs are made shapely by muscles. And those 'dinner ladies' arms are partly due to muscle loss. So looking after muscles makes men look like men but it also makes women look like women.

Fortunately, it's relatively easy to slow the decline, especially if you weren't exactly Mr or Mrs Universe in the first place. In fact, you could actually become stronger than you ever were: essentially, **all you have to do is exercise against a resistance.**

In the old days it used to be called *pumping iron,* but nowadays there are elegantly designed machines for use in trendy health clubs or at home.

Insight

Ladies, let me set your minds at rest straight away over the fear that you'll end up looking like Arnold Schwarzenegger. Arnie didn't get that way in two half-hour sessions a week. That required years of dedication, most days of the week, most hours of the day. You'll no more get like that than you'll win an Olympic marathon as a result of the jogging recommended earlier.

The best way to get started is to join a health club and use the machines under the supervision of a professional. Here are the advantages of health clubs:

▶ *It means you don't have to have any special equipment at home.*
▶ *You can use them whatever the weather.*
▶ *They can be visited alone or with friends.*
▶ *You can exercise a wide range of muscles as well as the heart/lungs.*

- ▶ *You get access to a professional who can advise and motivate you.*
- ▶ *Progress is very easy to measure.*
- ▶ *It is trendy!*

But:

- ▶ *You will require training before you can use the equipment safely.*
- ▶ *If the gym is a long way from home you may not always feel like going.*
- ▶ *Health clubs are expensive.*

Later, you might like to buy a machine for use at home. You gain in convenience – although one home machine can't exercise as many muscles as the range of machines in a health club.

Insight

More weight/resistance and fewer repetitions leads to more prominent-looking muscles. Less weight/resistance and frequent repetitions leads to elongated muscles.

Exercising for flexibility

Loss of flexibility is one of the most obvious signs of ageing. You might say you don't need to be flexible – after all, you're not a ballet dancer – but you'd be surprised. You start finding it difficult to put your shoes on. It's difficult to get into the car. It's even harder to get out of the car.

What you need is *stretching*.

Stretching is something that's difficult to learn from a book. The best thing is to take classes in, say, yoga, pilates, gymnastics, tai chi, aerobic dance or even one of the 'dance meditations' such as

5Rhythms. Once you've got the basics you can then either continue with the classes or exercise at home

---

Devising a weekly programme for fitness, strength and flexibility

Unless time is no object, aim to devote 30 minutes a day to your exercise programme. Because of the varied nature of the programme below it isn't necessary to have a rest day – but take one if you feel the need.

A useful way of dividing the week up would be:

Day 1: Fitness (jogging/cycling/swimming, etc.)
Day 2: Resistance training (weights/machines, etc.)
Day 3: Flexibility (yoga/aerobic dance, etc.)
Day 4: Fitness (jogging/cycling/swimming, etc.)
Day 5: Resistance training (weights/machines, etc.)
Day 6: Flexibility (yoga/aerobic dance, etc.)
Day 7: Fitness (jogging/cycling/swimming, etc.)

Top tips

Here are a few tips on keeping motivated:

▶ *Try to take your exercise at a certain time every day so that, when the time comes round, your body will soon start demanding that you do something active with it.*
▶ *If the weather is bad on a fitness day, switch to an indoor activity such as weight training or yoga.*
▶ *Exercise together with friends and jolly one another along (unless, of course, you prefer to be alone).*
▶ *Don't strain; take it easy and build up gradually.*

(Contd)

- ▶ *Keep an exercise diary and enter your distances, times, heart rates, scores or whatever; look at it from time to time and take pride in your progress.*
- ▶ *Give yourself rewards whenever you achieve a particular goal; if it's a cup you covet, then award yourself a cup – or it could be new clothes, a meal out, a massage or whatever you fancy (and can afford).*
- ▶ *Hang up a poster of your ideal body; remember, that's how you're going to look.*
- ▶ *Keep thinking of the health benefits – lower resting heart rate, blood pressure and weight, fewer health problems and up to four extra years of life.*

10 THINGS TO REMEMBER

1 *Exercise can increase your life by more than ten years.*

2 *Exercise makes you happy because it releases various happy chemicals including endorphins, phenylethylamine and noradrenaline/norepinephrine; it also lowers cortisol, the stress hormone.*

3 *Exercise can help you combat involutional melancholia or 'middle age depression' – it's recommended by the UK's National Institute for Health and Clinical Excellence (NICE).*

4 *You need to exercise not only for fitness but also for strength and flexibility.*

5 *For fitness, you should exercise at around 70 per cent of your Maximum Heart Rate (MHR).*

6 *Jogging, cycling and swimming are excellent ways of becoming fit.*

7 *Weight/resistance machines are the best for increasing strength.*

8 *Yoga, pilates, gymnastics, tai chi and certain dance styles are good for flexibility.*

9 *As a minimum, set aside 30 minutes a day for exercise.*

10 *If you're not used to exercise, consult a doctor before starting an exercise programme.*

HOW MUCH LONGER ARE YOU GOING TO LIVE NOW?

▶ *Have you succeeded in lowering your resting heart rate?*
▶ *Can you touch the floor with your legs straight?*
▶ *Have you increased the number of sit-ups you can do?*
▶ *Can you walk half a mile faster than you used to?*
▶ *Are you exercising regularly at your optimum training heart rate?*
▶ *Have you increased your strength, as proven by increased weights/resistance?*
▶ *Have you increased your flexibility?*
▶ *Have you devised a comprehensive all-weather exercise programme and are you sticking to it?*
▶ *Are you keeping an exercise diary?*
▶ *Have you devised a system of targets and rewards?*

Score:

If you answered 'yes' to seven or more questions you're obviously very serious about getting fitter and living longer. You'll be rewarded by a significant increase in your life expectancy as well as in your quality of life. Move on to the next chapter.

If you answered 'yes' to between four and six questions you're well on the way to fitness. You can also move on to the next chapter but re-read this one from time to time and keep adding to the range of your activities.

If you answered 'yes' to three or fewer questions you undoubtedly want to live longer (who doesn't?) but you're probably not convinced of the benefits of exercise. There's bound to be an activity over which you can enthuse, if only you can find it. Maybe it will help you to get together with a few friends to tackle something different each week. Try to get your score up to five 'yesses' before moving on.

5

Your brain

In this chapter you will learn:

* *how your brain and mind work*
* *the effects of ageing on your brain*
* *how to slow down age-related damage to your brain*
* *exercises to improve your memory.*

> *Education is the best provision for old age.*
>
> Aristotle

What's the point of going to school? You probably asked that question yourself when you were younger. No doubt you pointed to a pop singer who left school early, without any qualifications and went on to make a fortune. Your children and grandchildren, if you have any, will ask the same question.

Well, here are two very good and probably unexpected answers:

1 *The better educated you are* the longer you're likely to live.
2 *The better educated you are,* the less likely you are to suffer from dementia.

Those are facts that should get everyone enthusiastic about their homework.

To demonstrate the truth about the mental health benefits of education, researchers from the University of San Diego went to Shanghai. They wanted to find elderly people who had never had much education, and in the USA that was almost impossible. In China they studied more than 5,000 people aged over 75 and clearly showed that those with little education were *three times* more likely to have dementia than those with a higher education. Various studies all over the world have come to a similar conclusion. Why should that be?

In 1988 Robert Katzman and Robert Terry compared the brains of people who had died while suffering from Alzheimer's disease with a control group of people who had died without showing any signs of mental impairment. To their astonishment, they found the same Alzheimer's-type physical brain damage in many of the *control* group as in the Alzheimer's group.

Thus the 'reserve hypothesis' was born. It goes like this. Far from being a fixed lump that steadily loses cells over the years, the brain turns out to be more like a muscle. If you train it well, by getting a good education, you can increase its power and better withstand any subsequent 'muscle' damage. In other words, if your brain is 'strong' enough you can effectively have Alzheimer's without showing any symptoms.

That's pretty reassuring if you remained in formal education into your twenties. But supposing you didn't?

First the bad news. We know for sure that certain brain functions can never be recovered if they are not developed at the right moment. This applies mostly to the days and weeks after birth. A study of nuns found those who had had poor linguistic skills when young all developed Alzheimer's, whereas none of those with good linguistic skills in youth did. That seems to suggest that how you start out governs how you finish up.

Now for the good news. The linguistically challenged nuns probably didn't do as much to keep their brains active as their better-educated sisters. A lot of experiments with rats, and a few with people, have shown that the brain enjoys a certain amount of experience-dependent plasticity (EDP) throughout life. In other words, the brain is somewhat like the rest of your body. You're not going to get any taller as an adult but there's still plenty you can do to make your body fitter, stronger and more flexible. In the same way, how your brain ends up is also under your adult control in several ways. These include:

▶ *nutrition*
▶ *physical activity*
▶ *avoiding stress*
▶ *avoiding neurotoxicants*
▶ *avoiding head injury*
▶ *mental activity.*

A study in Japan, published in 1994, found five risk factors for Alzheimer's: psychosocial inactivity, physical inactivity, head injury, poor education and loss of teeth. Compared with people who had none of the risk factors, those with all five were *more than 900 times more likely to develop Alzheimer's.*

There's an obvious logic behind the first four but what on earth could be the connection with lost teeth? It's possible they signal a general lack of self-care, but it may be that periodontal disease, characterized by bleeding gums, is indicative of the poor vascular health that would be so damaging for the brain.

We'll be taking a look at the things you can do to keep your brain sharp in a moment, but first let's learn a little bit more about how our brains and minds work, and why they sometimes don't.

....

Insight

Sometimes low hormone levels can be responsible for failing memory and a lack of mental sharpness. A 1994 study of nearly 9,000 elderly women at Leisure World, a retirement community in California, found the longer a woman had used oestrogen replacement therapy, and the higher the dose, the lower the risk of Alzheimer's. Several studies since

(Contd)

have found the same, some of them showing the risk cut by as much as half. Declining testosterone levels can sometimes be a problem for both men and women. If you have concerns about your hormone levels, discuss them with your doctor.

How your brain works

Your brain is the part of your central nervous system that's located inside your skull. Identifying it is no mystery. Open up the skull and there it is, a big, wrinkly lump weighing around 1.4 kg (3 lb). As for your mind, well, that's something philosophers have argued about for centuries. The mystics say it's your sense of self. But a reasonable and concrete analogy would be that the brain is like computer hardware while the mind is like a combination of software and data. One thing's for sure – no brain, no mind. Or as neurologists like to say, there could be mindless brains but there are never brainless minds.

Here are some things about your brain you may not know:

- ▶ *At 20 weeks, your foetal brain attained its peak number of neurons (nerve cells) – 200 billion.*
- ▶ *Before you were born, 100 billion neurons that were defective 'committed suicide' in a process known as apoptosis.*
- ▶ *That left you with around 100 billion neurons at birth – and 100 trillion synapses (connections between neurons).*
- ▶ *Each of your neurons contains a cell body with a nucleus, a long extension called an axon, and many smaller extensions called dendrites.*
- ▶ *Messages are carried across synapses by chemicals known as neurotransmitters.*
- ▶ *The neurotransmitters are detected by receptors.*
- ▶ *The brain accounts for only 2 per cent of body weight but uses 20 per cent of the body's energy.*

Dementia

We've all heard of Alzheimer's disease and we're all terrified of our parents, our partners and ourselves getting it. It was named after Dr Alois Alzheimer who, in Frankfurt in 1901, treated a 51-year-old woman, suffering from extreme confusion, memory loss, hallucinations and delusions. There was little he could do for her but when she died four years later he examined her brain and found unhealthy formations known as plaques and tangles as well as a loss of neurons and clogged blood vessels. It's the plaques and tangles that are nowadays known as Alzheimer's.

Here are some facts about Alzheimer's:

▶ *Alzheimer's occurs in 3 per cent of people aged 65, 12 per cent of people aged 75, and half of those aged 85 and over.*
▶ *About half the risk of developing Alzheimer's is genetic and half is due to environmental factors.*

But, frightening though it is, we're all focusing too much on Alzheimer's simply because it has such a memorable name. What causes Alzheimer's is rather less important than what causes dementia – 'decline in mind' – generally. Alzheimer's is characterized by specific kinds of plaques and tangles, but there are others that are equally damaging, and many other horrible things that can happen to your brain. There's plenty of evidence, for example, that by the age of 30 some aspects of our brains are already in decline. So the important thing is to tackle all of the

problems associated with the ageing brain, not just Alzheimer's.
With an ageing brain:

▶ *neurons shrink*
▶ *the fatty insulation around the neurons thins*
▶ *the number of synapses declines (but existing synapses can be broadened)*
▶ *the chemistry of the brain changes*
▶ *mutations in mitochondrial DNA in the nucleus of each neuron accelerate, causing, among other things, more dangerous free radicals to be released (see page 15)*
▶ *senile plaques (SPs) and neurofibrillary tangles (NFTs) appear.*

This general deterioration is known as ageing-related neurodegeneration (ARN). And when it looks like Alzheimer's, but technically might not be, it's called ageing-related neurodegeneration of the Alzheimer's type (ARNAT). ARN is the most rapidly growing cause of death in the USA. It's partly because more people are living long enough to suffer ARN, but also partly due to new environmental factors.

ARN doesn't affect all brain functions equally:

▶ *The slowest decline is in crystallized intelligence – information we use repeatedly, such as general knowledge, words and practical skills.*
▶ *The fastest decline is in fluid intelligence – the ability to deal with new information, spatial reasoning, problem solving and information processing.*

What can we do to put the brake on these changes and even throw them into reverse?

Insight

Scientists have long recognized that people with rheumatoid arthritis are less likely to develop Alzheimer's disease. It was thought the frequent use of anti-inflammatory drugs might be the explanation. But in 2010 it was discovered that rheumatoid arthritis itself triggered the body's natural production of a protein called GM-CSF (Granulocyte-Macrophage Colony Stimulating Factor). When this protein was given to mice with artificially induced Alzheimer's it completely reversed cognitive impairment in 20 days. It so happens that the same protein is already in production as the chemical sargramostim (trade name Leukine) to boost white blood cells during cancer treatment. Human trials for its use in Alzheimer's were due to begin at the time of writing.

NUTRITION

Basically, your brain needs 'food', just like the rest of your body. Brain food is oxygen and glucose. If it doesn't get enough – and, remember, the brain needs 20 per cent of the body's energy – the neurons suffer.

Many of the reasons a brain doesn't get enough blood, and therefore oxygen and glucose, are to do with faulty nutrition. This can cause:

▶ *arteriosclerosis*
▶ *strokes*
▶ *diabetes.*

ARTERIOSCLEROSIS

Arteriosclerosis is the deposition of a kind of fat called cholesterol on the walls of the arteries, making them stiff and reducing the blood flow. That's exactly what you don't want for a healthy brain. **Nutritional risk factors** for arteriosclerosis include:

▶ *high sugar intake*
▶ *high fat intake*
▶ *inadequate vitamin intake*

- *diabetes (which, as we'll see in a moment, may be linked to nutrition)*
- *hypertension (which may also be linked to poor nutrition).*

Other risk factors for arteriosclerosis include:

- *stress*
- *smoking*
- *inactivity*
- *infection with chlamydia pneumoniae.*

STROKES

A stroke is the cutting off of oxygen to a region of the brain for sufficiently long – a couple of minutes will do it – for cells to die. Strokes come in two forms:

- **Ischemic** – *meaning 'too little blood', the result of a blood vessel becoming blocked.*
- **Haemorrhagic** – *the result of a blood vessel bursting.*

Ischemic strokes are by far the most common. The way the blockage usually happens is this. A cholesterol-filled plaque on the wall of an artery will continue to build up and up until it finally ruptures. When it does so, blood platelets, mistaking the rupture for a rupture in the blood vessel itself, stick all over it and risk blocking the artery itself. Meanwhile, the yellow muck (the plaque) may be carried along in the blood until it reaches a narrow place where it lodges and effectively dams up the blood vessel. It could be anywhere. Sometimes it happens in the eye. Sometimes it happens in the brain. When it's in the brain it's called a stroke and its effect depends on where in the brain the blockage occurs. Nutritional risk factors for ischemic strokes include:

- *high total cholesterol*
- *high levels of 'bad' LDL cholesterol relative to 'good' HDL cholesterol*
- *hypertension (elevated blood pressure).*

Hypertension

As you've probably noticed, hypertension is associated with both arteriosclerosis and strokes. What's more, various studies have shown that hypertension itself, even without a stroke, seems to lower mental performance. For example, a study of more than 2,000 French people found that those with high systolic pressure (the upper level) performed less well in cognitive tests than those with normal systolic pressure. A 20-year Swedish study of a thousand men with high diastolic pressure (the lower level) found that by age 70 they had lower mental performance than other men. And a British study of men with high blood pressure found they performed less well in just about every cognitive function than men with normal blood pressure.

Nutritional risk factors include:

▶ *high cholesterol (see page 20)*
▶ *high salt consumption (only in some salt-sensitive people)*
▶ *obesity*
▶ *diabetes (see page 112)*
▶ *high alcohol consumption (see pages 181–183).*

Other risk factors include:

- ▶ *inactivity (see page 115 and Chapter 4)*
- ▶ *stress (see pages 132–134)*
- ▶ *smoking (see pages 176–180)*
- ▶ *a tendency in the family to suffer hypertension.*

DIABETES

A study of over 6,000 elderly people in Holland found that those with diabetes were almost twice as likely as non-diabetics to have Alzheimer's. And various other studies have confirmed the link.

There are four ways that diabetes can harm your brain:

1 *It reduces the ability of brain cells to take in glucose.*
2 *It damages blood vessels, including the tiny blood vessels deep inside the brain.*
3 *It seems to cause damage to proteins in the brain, just as is seen in Alzheimer's disease.*
4 *It starves brain cells of fuel whenever you suffer a low (from administering too much insulin).*

There are two kinds of diabetes:

- ▶ **Type 1** – *this usually occurs in children and young adults and seems to be an autoimmune disorder in which the body attacks the pancreas and prevents it from producing insulin. Type 1 accounts for only 10 per cent of diabetes or less and is not related to diet.*
- ▶ **Type 2** – *this usually occurs in adults and is initially caused by the failure of the cells to respond to insulin (but, later, may also involve the failure of the pancreas as it struggles to produce more and more insulin). Type 2 is related to faulty nutrition and is the type we're concerned with here.*

The way to lower the risk of Type 2 diabetes is to:

▶ *avoid or minimize foods that quickly raise blood sugar.
These include sugar itself, honey and refined carbohydrates
such as white flour and white rice.*
▶ *avoid getting overweight. Why? Because fat cells release a
hormone that makes other cells insulin-resistant. Insulin-
resistance in turn means that cells can't take up glucose.
Glucose is the fuel used by brain cells, which therefore suffer
and eventually die.*

Insight

We've all heard of insulin but what exactly is it? It's a
hormone that controls everything to do with the energy –
that is, the glucose – in your body. When you eat, the level
of sugar in your blood rises. Your pancreas then releases
insulin which transports the glucose to your cells. Any excess
glucose is stored in the liver and muscles as glycogen. When
those stores are full, if there's still an excess, it's converted to
fat. A problem arises when, over the years, you consistently
eat too much of the kind of food that quickly raises your
blood sugar to excessive levels. The pancreas has to pump out
huge quantities of insulin and, over time, the cells become, as
it were, fatigued and develop insulin resistance. Your body
can no longer use energy efficiently and you're on your way
to full Type 2 diabetes.

Try this

There's a very simple way of reducing your risk of diabetes. Lose
weight. That's not to say slim people don't get diabetes. They do.
But their risk is much lower. All you have to do to lower your risk
to theirs is eat a little less and exercise a little more. In one study
of 3,000 overweight people, a combination of diet and a brisk
walk five days a week was as effective as an anti-diabetes drug.
As little as a 5 per cent weight loss could be enough to make all
the difference.

Yes, it's easy to say and much harder to do. But these simple rules could make all the difference:

Step 1: Assess what you're eating to see if there are things you could easily cut out. For example, do you always have a biscuit with a cup of tea or coffee?

Step 2: Stop adding sugar to drinks and stop sprinkling it on things like cereals and fruits. Your drinks will taste horrible for a day or two but after that you won't even notice the difference.

Step 3: Avoid eating refined carbohydrates, which release energy quickly. In other words, substitute equivalent whole foods which release energy slowly, such as wholemeal bread for white bread, brown rice for white rice, whole grains for commercial breakfast cereals and so on.

Step 4: Reduce your use of processed foods – they often contain sugar.

Step 5: Choose lean meat rather than more fatty meats.

Step 6: Substitute fruit for sweet puddings.

Just look at the difference these simple steps could make without taking away any of the pleasure in your meals.

Action	Calories saved per day
Cutting out six biscuits	300
Cutting out ten teaspoons of sugar	200
Substituting fresh for processed foods	100
Substituting lean meat for fat meat	200
Substituting fruit for pudding	200
Total	1,000

If you actually did cut out 1,000 calories a day you'd lose roughly 2 pounds or almost 1 kilo a week. In fact, that would be too drastic. The best course is to get your weight down *gradually* over one or two years. As you can see, it doesn't have to take a lot of willpower or discomfort. Get started by eliminating that unnecessary sugar and carry on from there.

....

Insight

These are the essential nutrients in the brain diet:

- ▶ *The B group vitamins for healthy nerves.*
- ▶ *Vitamins C and E for healthy blood vessels.*
- ▶ *Iron for transporting oxygen to the brain.*
- ▶ *Calcium: essential for communication between neurons.*
- ▶ *Chocolate: contains various brain-saving chemicals.*
- ▶ *Tea: reduces the risk of strokes.*
- ▶ *Red wine: various studies suggest light drinking (see pages 29–30) lowers the risk of dementia. But heavy drinking kills brain cells.*
- ▶ *Omega-3 fatty acids: found in oily fish and flaxseed oil and in smaller quantities in rapeseed oil (canola) and walnuts, they protect against heart disease, arthritis and possibly cancer.*

For more details re-read Chapters 2 and 3.

....

Physical activity

Exercise promotes longevity. It also promotes a healthy brain. In one study, for example, highly active people had only half the rate of Alzheimer's of inactive people. High levels of fitness are also associated with better ability to learn new things as well as fast reaction times. And if you want to increase your IQ, getting fit will help that, too. Exercise:

- ▶ *helps prevent arteriosclerosis*
- ▶ *helps maintain cerebral blood flow*
- ▶ may *boost neuronal growth (it certainly does in rats)*
- ▶ *reduces the risk of stroke.*

So if you haven't already begun an exercise programme, re-read Chapter 4 and get going.

Avoiding stress

Stress is a huge problem for the body and for longevity and is dealt with in detail in Chapter 6. Here we'll just concentrate on the effect of stress on the brain.

When you're stressed, the adrenal cortex (the outer layer of the adrenal gland) pumps out stress hormones known as glucocorticoids (GCs). They have perfectly beneficial functions, including helping the brain to remember. The idea is that you'll recognize and avoid that stress in the future. But if you're almost constantly stressed they have a terrible long-term side effect. They, possibly together with another stress chemical known as corticotropin releasing factor (CRF), damage and can even kill your neurons.

There's plenty of evidence for this. For example, scans of the brains of adults suffering post-traumatic stress disorder (PTSD) as a result of childhood abuse revealed 12 per cent atrophy of the part of the brain known as the left hippocampus. In the case of PTSD-afflicted Vietnam veterans, the atrophy was far worse: a savage 26 per cent. That effectively means the loss of millions of memory cells. And those were young people at the time of the traumas. Older people and those already suffering a degree of dementia seem to be even worse affected. The message is clear: *stress harms the brain*.

If you want to know what you can do about it, see Chapter 6.

Avoiding neurotoxicants

All around us there are substances that are poisonous to the brain. A lot of them are man-made (toxicants) and a few occur naturally (toxins). One of the most potentially dangerous is aluminium, which can damage proteins in the brain.

And yet, worryingly, we're surrounded by aluminium. It's the third most common element in the earth's crust. It's in water. It's in food. In some areas, it's in the air we breathe. And it's in some medicines. So why aren't we all suffering aluminium-related dementia? Clearly, the problem of aluminium isn't quite as simple as it seems.

One of the complications is that aluminium comes in various different forms, some of which may be dangerous and others not. What's more, the body has mechanisms for keeping neurotoxins and neurotoxicants out of the brain. Some people may be better at that than others.

Until more is known it makes sense to avoid aluminium as much as possible:

▶ *Don't use aluminium cooking pots.*
▶ *Avoid antiperspirants containing aluminium.*
▶ *Avoid calcium supplements marked 'natural source' or 'oyster shell' which may contain aluminium – use other kinds.*
▶ *Limit antacids that contain aluminium.*
▶ *Ask your water authority to tell you the aluminium content of your water supply – if it exceeds 200 mcg/l install a reverse-osmosis unit or drink bottled water.*
▶ *If you need dialysis, check that your hospital is taking all precautions against aluminium poisoning.*

Here are a few more brain poisons to be wary of:

▶ *pesticides*
▶ *solvents*
▶ *arsenic*
▶ *lead*
▶ *manganese*
▶ *mercury*
▶ *thallium.*

Always take proper precautions when handling brain poisons.

Avoiding head injury

Our brains are encased inside a pretty tough layer of bone, so it may seem that nature has done enough. Indeed, in the sort of world in which humans evolved it normally was enough. But today's world is very different. Back then, you couldn't go faster than you could run. In the next stage, you couldn't go faster than a horse could run. Now we have all kinds of ways of travelling at enormous speed – bicycles, skis, motorbikes, cars, planes and all the rest. The skull alone is no longer any kind of protection. In fact, it's the skull that is often the *cause* of brain injury. In any sudden deceleration, such as a car hitting a wall, your skull stops moving but your brain keeps on going. The temporal lobes of the brain hit the sharp temporal bone *inside* the skull and the frontal lobes slam into the frontal bones. Not good.

In one study, the rate of head trauma among Alzheimer's victims was found to be ten times higher than normal for the age group.

The message is: wear a top-quality helmet whenever appropriate.

For more information, see pages 187–188.

Mental activity

Does the 'use it or lose it' principle apply to the brain? All the evidence suggests that it certainly does. And the best way to use it is as *comprehensively* as possible. In other words, concentrating on one type of mental exercise (such as a crossword puzzle) isn't enough. You need to exercise *every* aspect of your brain to get the maximum benefit.

Here are some suggestions and exercises to help you do just that.

IMPROVING YOUR MEMORY

Every day you collect the post. Some of it is junk and you throw it away. Some of it is important and you store it in your filing system. The brain is exactly the same. It has a *short-term* memory, which allows you to read this sentence and remember enough of the beginning to understand the end. But you won't remember it in five minutes unless it's been put into *long-term* storage. And the brain only does that when it has a very good reason.

What's a good reason? Anything that threatens your life is a good reason. Your brain automatically stores the data so you'll be able to recognize the threat next time. But when that sort of stimulation is lacking, what can you do?

Concentrate
Research suggests it takes eight seconds of concentration to process a piece of information through to a memory centre.

Repetition, repetition, repetition
If you are old enough you'll remember learning things 'parrot fashion' at school. Unfortunately for later generations, the technique went out of use. But the fact is that repetition is far from mindless. On the contrary, it's one of the best ways of convincing your brain of the importance of the information. In which case, your brain will put it into long-term storage.

Rehearse
Once you've got the information into your long-term memory, rehearse it from time to time. On the first day, rehearse it several times and on subsequent days rehearse it at least once until you're confident.

Association
What do you do when you have a piece of paper that doesn't belong in any of the files you've created? Let me guess. You put in your in-tray, or something like that, and leave it for the next time.

Well, the brain is a bit like that, too. It likes to know where to file information. When something completely new comes along it sometimes doesn't know what to do with it, because you haven't created a file.

This is where association comes in. In other words, you link new information with something you already know. Then you can store and retrieve it more easily. One technique for learning lists by association (also known as the 'method of loci') is to imagine walking along a street you're very familiar with. You then assign each item on the list to a particular spot or building.

Let's say, for example, you need to remember some names. How about Rosemary Barnes? Easy! She's the garden with the rose bushes and, for good measure, you imagine the roses growing up the side of a barn. The next house with the unusual green roof is Jim Tyler. The pond in the garden is Anne Salmon. And so on.

Use all your senses
Most of us learn best when we can see something. It's harder to remember a name we're told than it is when we can see it written down. But it's easiest of all when we can see something and hear it and relate it to our other senses. So if you're reading something you need to remember, then, also:

- ▶ *say it out loud*
- ▶ *write it*
- ▶ *draw it, if possible*
- ▶ *try to attribute a colour, smell, texture or taste to it.*

Use a mnemonic device
A mnemonic (don't pronounce the initial 'm') is anything that helps us remember. The association technique (above) is one style of mnemonic, but there are others:

- ▶ **Rhymes:** *A well-known example is, 'Thirty days hath September…'*

- **Acronyms:** *These are initials that create words or memorable sounds. For example, to remember North Atlantic Treaty Organization you only have to recall NATO.*
- **Sentences:** *These can be constructed so that the initial letter of each word reminds you of what you want to remember. 'Every good boy deserves food', for example, is a reminder that the notes E, G, B, D and F are written on the stave lines in the treble clef.*
- **Chunks:** *When numbers are too long it helps to break them up into sub-groups of three. For example, 982438657 is hard to remember but 982 438 657 is easier.*
- **Visual images:** *These work by simple association. For example, to remember the name 'Sue' you might think of a courtroom, or to remember the name 'Derek' you might envisage an oil well.*

Insight

If you don't expect to be able to remember something, then you probably won't. Be confident in your abilities and your brain will respond.

Increasing your brain power

Unless you're going to be applying for a job you're probably not very interested in knowing what your intelligence quotient (IQ) is. But, in fact, IQ tests are a good way of keeping tabs on your mental abilities and, indeed, improving them. Half your IQ is linked to your genes and there's nothing you can do about that. But the other half is under your control. In other words, IQ is *not* fixed. Whatever your IQ is today you can increase it.

You can do this in a number of ways, for example:

- *Healthy diet: Add four points.*
- *Having regular, reasoned debates and conversations: Add six points.*

- ▶ *Relaxation and preparation: Add 14 points.*
- ▶ *Proper sleep: Add 15 points.*

Of course, you'll only enjoy those increases if you were already completely deficient in those things. But all of us probably have some room for improvement in our habits and when you consider that the average IQ is, by definition, 100, such changes could be highly significant.

Probably the best way to increase your IQ is simply to do IQ tests regularly. You'll come to understand the style of thinking and generally improve the necessary skills. What's more, if you do go on to take an IQ test as part of a job application you'll probably find questions similar to the ones you've already done in your practice sessions.

Here are some examples of the kinds of questions you need to be able to get to grips with.

Q1 Eight small squares

Remove four lines to leave eight small squares.

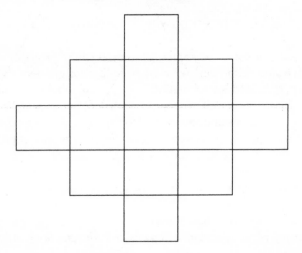

Q2 What time is it Mr Wolf?

Which clock, A, B, C, or D, completes the series?

Series

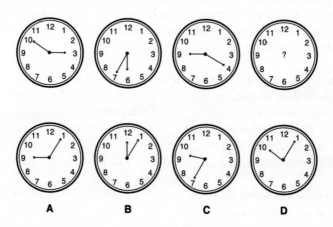

A   B   C   D

Q3 Stacking pyramids

Move three lines only to make five triangles.

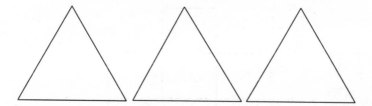

Q4 Eternal triangles

Add three lines to make eight triangles.

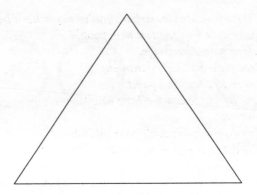

Q5 The one-match trick

Move one match to balance the equation.

(Answers at the end of the chapter.)

Here's a list of some of the things you can do to exercise your mind and build new synapses. Don't select just one. Aim to do all of them – and more.

▶ *Take a holiday somewhere you've never been before.*
▶ *Make an effort to meet new people.*
▶ *Learn a new language.*
▶ *Practise a musical instrument.*
▶ *Learn to draw and paint.*
▶ *Learn how to work all the new technology in your house properly.*
▶ *Try doing things with your other hand.*
▶ *Try doing things in the dark.*
▶ *Invent new words.*
▶ *Write a new ending for a well-known story or some new stanzas for a well-known poem.*
▶ *Be creative; try to think in new and original ways.*
▶ *Cultivate curiosity.*
▶ *Be open to new ideas; don't insist on doing things the way you always did them.*

10 THINGS TO REMEMBER

1 *The better your education the longer you're likely to live and the lower your risk of dementia, because education creates a 'reserve' of power making the brain better able to withstand ageing.*

2 *Your brain enjoys experience-dependent plasticity (EDP) throughout your life which means it's never too late to improve your education, formal or informal.*

3 *Declining hormone levels can affect memory and mental performance.*

4 *Your brain is analogous to computer hardware while your mind is analogous to the computer software and data.*

5 *It's a myth that you lose large numbers of neurons as you age (in fact, it's possible to add new neurons as an adult) but they do shrink.*

6 *The fastest decline is in fluid intelligence and the slowest is in crystallized intelligence – keep mentally active, especially by trying new things.*

7 *Good nutrition is essential for a healthy brain; arteriosclerosis, strokes and Type 2 diabetes are all brain-threatening conditions related to incorrect nutrition.*

8 *Exercise is essential for a healthy brain, but take care to avoid head injuries – wear a helmet whenever appropriate.*

9 *Stress is damaging to the brain.*

10 *Neurotoxicants such as aluminium and pesticides should be avoided or handled with care.*

HOW MUCH LONGER ARE YOU GOING TO LIVE NOW?

- ▶ *Are you taking good care of your teeth and gums?*
- ▶ *Have you discussed hormone replacement with your doctor?*
- ▶ *Are you eating 'brain food' and avoiding 'brain poisons'?*
- ▶ *Are you keeping your total cholesterol and LDL cholesterol levels down?*
- ▶ *Are you keeping away from foods that cause a rapid rise in blood sugar?*
- ▶ *Are you exercising regularly?*
- ▶ *Are you avoiding stress?*
- ▶ *Are you avoiding neurotoxicants?*
- ▶ *Do you wear a helmet when appropriate (cycling, riding, skiing, etc.)?*
- ▶ *Are you challenging yourself mentally over a wide range of different skills?*

Score:

If you answered 'yes' to seven or more questions you're obviously very serious about keeping your brain as fit as possible as the years go by. You'll be rewarded by a quality of life better than it would have been otherwise. Move on to the next chapter.

If you answered 'yes' to between four and six questions you're well on the way to maintaining mental fitness but you should try to do a bit more. You can also move on to the next chapter but re-read this one from time to time and try to follow further recommendations.

If you answered 'yes' to three or fewer questions you undoubtedly want to keep mentally fit throughout life (who doesn't?) but maybe you're not convinced these things will help. Well, why not try them anyway? You have nothing to lose and everything to gain. Keep working on this chapter and don't move on until your score is at least four 'yesses'.

Q1

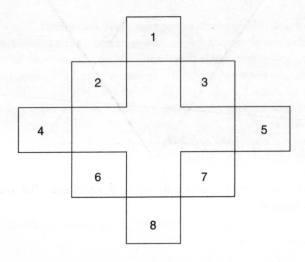

Q2 B (hour hand moving 15 minutes clockwise, minute hand moving 15 minutes anti-clockwise).

Q3

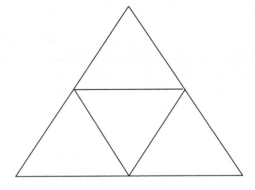

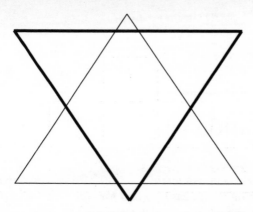

Q5 Move one match from equals sign and place it parallel to the
minus sign.

6

....

Relaxation

In this chapter you will learn:
- *why taking things easy is good for you*
- *how stress can cause health problems*
- *various techniques for overcoming stress and feeling relaxed.*

In 1908, a German scientist by the name of Max Rubner came to the rather astonishing conclusion that every animal had a specific amount of what might be called 'life energy'. When the energy was used up the animal died. It sounded crazy and no one took much notice. A few decades later another scientist called Roland Prinzinger came to the same conclusion. He called his discovery Metabolic Theory. He even succeeded in calculating the figure. It was 2,500 kilojoules of energy per gram of body weight. Again most people forgot. But in the last few years the whole idea has been resurrected, especially by Roy Walford, the late American specialist on ageing, whom we met in Chapter 2.

There's plenty of anecdotal evidence and more than a modicum of logic to support the idea. For example, worker bees, which live at a frenzied pace, die within three to six months whereas the inactive queen bee usually lives five years or even more. Animals in zoos live far longer than their counterparts in the wild. Polar bears, for example, live around 20 years in the Arctic but 40 years in zoos, while lions live ten years on the plains of Africa and 20 years in captivity. Of course, there are other factors at work but the indolent life of a zoo inmate could have quite a lot to do with it.

The message, then, is *relax* and don't burn more energy than you have to. How does that square with the almost universal advice to exercise? In fact, as we saw in Chapter 4, it matches perfectly. When you're fit your heart beats a whole lot slower and, overall, you actually burn far less energy. The trick is not to overdo it. The amount of exercise recommended in Chapter 4 seems about right in terms of Metabolic Theory. The rest of the time, take it easy.

The slow movement

When McDonald's announced it was going to open a restaurant in Rome's Piazza di Spagna in the late 1980s there was an immediate protest, led by a food and wine writer called Carlo Petrini. And thus the International Slow Food Movement was born. In Paris in 1989 more than 20 delegations from all over the world signed a manifesto promoting 'the richness and aromas of local cuisine' and proclaiming 'Slow Food' as the cutting-edge answer to the 'Fast Life'.

As befits such a philosophy, the Slow Food Movement has grown, well, slowly, but also inexorably. Carlo Petrini is now hailed as a kind of guru by many, including Prince Charles and Al Gore. For him, the most important things about food are every day to 'eat dinner with the one you love', and to use traditional, local ingredients produced in a way that 'does not harm the environment, animal welfare or our health'.

Food remains the central concern but, bit by bit, new campaigns have been added and now there's slow *everything* from sightseeing to sex. All very good advice for living longer.

Here are some ideas for taking life more slowly:

▶ *Limit the number of things you try to accomplish in a day; just concentrate on the most important ones.*
▶ *Don't confuse action with movement. In other words, it's possible to rush around without achieving very much. Instead, focus on results.*

- *Eat meals sitting at a table, without watching TV – enjoy conversation instead.*
- *Aim to work and play close to home – don't assume the things furthest away are the most exciting.*
- *Throw away your watch – or, at least, don't wear one at weekends.*
- Savour *whatever you do – don't be thinking ahead to the next thing.*

Good and bad stress

What exactly is stress and why is it bad for us? Dictionaries define it as mental, emotional or physical strain, or something like that. But the specialists tend to see things differently. They talk in terms of good stress and bad stress. Or, as they put it, *eustress* and *distress*. How, you might ask, can stress ever be good?

Well, eustress might be when you try to clinch a business deal, for example, or try to ski down a slope a little bit steeper than you've tackled before. If you find these situations make you come alive, if your eyes shine, if you feel confident you can pull it off, then that's good stress. But if you feel weighed down, if your heart pounds so hard you fear your ribs will break, if you don't feel up to it, then that's bad stress.

You'll notice two different elements. There's the situation itself. And then there's your response to the situation. Let's go back to the ski slope. Two people are standing at the top. One is exhilarated by the challenge. That's eustress. The other is terrified. That's distress. And yet it's the same slope for both of them. The only difference is in their mental attitudes. One is confident of being able to cope. The other isn't.

Experiencing bad stress now and then isn't going to do you any harm. It's unavoidable at times. But a constant barrage of bad stress is damaging to your health and can take years off your life. So how can you convert distress into eustress?

Here's a bit of a paradox. The way to have confidence in your ability to cope is to constantly face up to new challenges. Yes, it's a bit Kafkaesque, isn't it? You don't want to be stressed. And, yet, in order not to be stressed you have to face stress! The solution to the paradox, of course, is that each new challenge should only take you a *little* bit beyond what you've achieved before. Gradually, step by step, over the months and years you reach a stage at which you know you can cope with almost *anything*.

In other words, if you're not yet ready for that difficult black slope, challenge yourself with harder and harder lines on the easier red slope. Then when you finally get to the top of the black you'll feel that invigorating eustress, not distress.

What is it about distress that's so harmful? In fact, the mechanism is well understood. The body responds to stress, as evolution has designed it to, by instantly preparing for 'fight or flight':

- *The adrenal glands release adrenaline and noradrenaline.*
- *The adrenal cortex releases stress hormones, including cortisol.*
- *Heart rate increases.*
- *Blood pressure rises.*
- *Blood moves from the internal organs to the muscles.*
- *Blood vessels in the skin constrict.*
- *Breathing deepens.*
- *Fuel (sugar and fat) pours into the bloodstream.*

All this is exactly as you'd want it to be if you're going to fight or run away from a sabre-toothed tiger. But if, as is the case for most of us nowadays, you're just going to sit there in your car, or at your desk, or in the waiting area, it's a disaster for your body. Here are some of the disorders and diseases associated with long-term stress-related changes:

- *coronary heart disease*
- *hypertension*
- *strokes*

- *cancers*
- *headaches and migraines*
- *heartburn*
- *ulcers*
- *neck and back pain*
- *rheumatoid arthritis*
- *allergies*
- *colds and flu*
- *anxiety and depression*
- *dementia (see previous chapter).*

The reasons are these. First of all, you have higher levels of fat in your blood, to provide the fuel for fight or flight. When you do neither, the blood remains thicker, more viscous and less able to flow along the small blood vessels, thus straining the heart. At the same time, some of the fat that isn't burned in physical activity may be deposited on the walls of your arteries as plaque, causing hypertension and a susceptibility to strokes. Similarly, high levels of the other fuel, sugar, can lead to diabetes. The increase in stomach acid causes heartburn. The cortisol suppresses the immune system, creating susceptibility to colds, flu, cancers and other diseases. The muscle tension causes headaches, neck and back pain. And the mental stress can result in anxiety and depression. It has to be emphasized that all this may be the result of chronic stress and not, of course, the occasional incident.

What can you do about it? One simple remedy is to exercise every time you get stressed. Pace up and down in your office. Go for a brisk walk or jog. Something like that. Then you're doing what nature intended. But, of course, that isn't always practical.

The only other solutions are to:

- *change your* situation
- *change your* mental attitude *to the situation.*

We'll be looking at those two options in the rest of this chapter.

Downsizing

Downsizing is one way in which you might change your *situation* so you don't have to change your *mental attitude* (although changing both together might be even better).

Downsizing comes about when you decide you just can't cope any more with the sort of pressures you used to cope with. Downsizing is something you do in middle age. Downsizing is deciding you no longer need the big salary, the big house, the big car and all the rest of it. It obviously works best if you can cash in your former life, as it were, and walk away with some capital to fund your new low-earning lifestyle. Because one thing's for sure: if you miscalculate and your new low income doesn't cover your new lower expenses, then you're very likely to keep on being stressed.

Insight

I (and my partner) downsized quite a few years ago. We've never regretted it. Looking back I can honestly say that when we downsized the most – living in a mountain hut that would have been condemned in a town – we were perfectly happy.

Relaxation techniques

Of course, there are stressful situations in life that just can't be avoided. So when they come along what can you do to minimize their impact on your health and longevity?

Over time, stress can cause physical changes to your body, including your brain. It's very important to understand that. Some of those changes may not be reversible. That's why it's so important to avoid stress damage.

Meditation

You may think that meditation is a load of Oriental mumbo jumbo. Well, in fact, it's backed by good scientific evidence. It works. Millions of people in the West practise some form of meditation and feel more relaxed as a result.

What exactly is it? There are many different styles and every 'guru' gives a different definition. Perhaps the most important aspect of meditation is learning to take control of both the conscious and subconscious mind. We all know, for example, what it's like to be tortured by those pointless worries that seem to come out of nowhere – especially in the middle of the night. Well, when you've reached a high level of skill in meditation you can put a stop to all that.

More technically, meditation means entering a state of consciousness that is neither the normal, everyday state of being awake nor the state of being asleep. There are four categories of brain waves, of which two are normally associated with meditation:

1 **Beta:** *13–40 Hz. The fastest frequencies, associated with normal waking consciousness and being alert.*
2 **Alpha:** *7–13 Hz. The next fastest frequencies, associated with feeling relaxed, daydreaming, reverie and light meditation.*
3 **Theta:** *4–7 Hz. Slower again, associated with dreaming sleep and deep meditation.*
4 **Delta:** *Under 4 Hz. The slowest, associated with deep sleep.*

Notice the use of the word 'associated' because, in fact, it's possible for two or three or even four frequencies to be present at the same time. Although 'light' meditation is normally said to be in alpha mode and 'deep' meditation in theta mode, in practice, deep meditation can involve not just alpha but also beta and theta and, in rare cases, all four. That is normally the preserve of a 'master' possessing what some call 'the awakened mind'. But everyone who meditates will combine frequencies in a way that is different from sleeping.

Apart from control of the mind, meditation has quite a few other benefits, including:

▶ *helping you experience inner happiness*
▶ *revitalizing you after your day's work*
▶ *cultivating a calmer mind and a more tranquil outlook*
▶ *lowering blood pressure*
▶ *improving the cardiovascular system*
▶ *enhancing immune function.*

In shallow souls, even the fish of small things can cause a commotion. In oceanic minds, the largest fish makes hardly a ripple.

Hindu proverb

HOW TO MEDITATE

So let's get started. The first thing is to sort out a time and place you can meditate. As a beginner you're probably best to have a quiet place where you won't be disturbed. Except for open-eyed styles of meditation, it will help if the room is dim or even dark or you could wear an eye mask. Make it a nice place so that you look forward to going to it and come to associate it with meditation.

As for the time of day, some teachers recommend first thing in the morning, especially before dawn, as a way of setting you up for the day. Others recommend the late evening, when everything has been done, as a way of unwinding from the day. Still others like to meditate at the end of the working day.

Find out what works best for you and then try to stick to it. Your body and mind will adapt accordingly and you'll find it increasingly easy to get into a meditative state when you go to your 'special place' at the same time every day.

The next thing to sort out is the position. It certainly isn't essential to sit in the lotus or even the half-lotus. Sitting cross-legged is fine. However you choose to sit, though, it's important that you make sure you keep your spine straight – don't slouch.

Rest your hands on your knees. One way is with the palms up and the thumb and forefinger of each hand touching to form an 'O'.

> **Insight**
>
> Here are a couple of tips I've found helpful. The first is to warm up by sitting on the floor with the soles of your feet together and close to your groin. Clasp your feet with your hands and move your knees up and down like a bird's wings. The second is to place a cushion under the rear of your buttocks to tip you forwards slightly and thus bring your knees down to the floor.

There are two alternatives to sitting on the floor. You can meditate perfectly well sitting on a dining chair or even an office swivel chair. The key element is to sit away from the back of the chair, keeping a straight spine. Just place your hands, palms down, lightly on your knees. The other alternative is to lie down. Many teachers frown on this as not being 'proper' and because of the danger of falling asleep. But, in fact, it's an excellent position for meditating because it automatically reduces beta waves. As with the other positions the spine must be straight, so lie on your back with your arms by your sides, palms up, and your feet shoulder width apart. To overcome the danger of falling asleep try lying on the floor rather than the bed so you don't get *too* comfortable.

The important thing, really, is the meditation not the pose. Whatever works for you is fine.

So you're sitting or lying down in a quiet place. Now what? Different people use different techniques and again you need to experiment to find out what works best for you. Some people, for example, stare at a candle flame or an image or a wall, others repeat mantras, still others repeat small almost imperceptible gestures.

Here's a simple way:

- *In your chosen position, smile. (Just make it a little 'secret' smile – as you might if a child did something funny but you didn't want to be seen laughing.)*
- *Gradually slow down your breathing, making your exhalations longer than your inhalations. Count, say, seven for an inhalation and 11 for an exhalation. Hold your breath for a few seconds in between.*
- *Let your mouth open and your tongue flop out.*
- *Empty your mind of any thoughts of past or future.*
- *Just concentrate on experiencing the present moment which is your breath.*
- *If any thoughts push their way into your mind just let them drift past; don't pursue them.*
- *When your breathing is slow and relaxed, notice your heartbeat.*
- *Without forcing anything, gradually try to think it slower.*
- *Next notice the sound of your blood in your ears.*
- *Without forcing anything, gradually try to think it slower.*
- *Now notice the little dots that 'illuminate' the blackness of your closed eyes.*
- *Imagine the dots are stars. Pick on one and head towards it...*

Insight

Using your left hand, try touching the tip of your ring finger against the fleshy base of your thumb as you breathe in and moving it away as you breathe out. As you breathe in think 'So' and as you breathe out think 'Hum'. It's a classic mantra which literally translates as 'I am That' but which, in effect, means 'I am part of the Divine Consciousness'. Some people find it goes better to say it the other way around ('Hum' as you breathe in, 'So' as you breathe out). It really doesn't make much difference.

You should now be meditating. But are you? Here are the stages you should go through:

- **Stage 1:** *Your mind is no longer filled with everyday matters and you sense that you're drifting towards sleep; you're on the very fringe of the meditative state.*

- **Stage 2:** *As you go deeper, images may come at you from nowhere. You don't actually fall asleep but start to feel as if you're floating. You may feel like rocking and swaying; that's fine at this stage but you'll need to stop moving to go deeper.*
- **Stage 3:** *You become intensely aware of the functioning of your body – breathing, heartbeat, blood flow – but at the same time you no longer know where your body ends and other things begin. Parts of your body may feel very heavy.*
- **Stage 4:** *You feel 'spaced out' and quite detached but, at the same time, alert.*
- **Stage 5:** *You feel in touch with the universe and nothing else matters at all.*

You could meditate all day. But, in the context of a busy modern life 20 to 30 minutes is the sort of time to aim for. The longer you can devote to it the more likely you are to reach a deep state. The profoundest meditative states are usually only reached by those who have been practising for a long time – perhaps two or three years. But you may occasionally experience moments of those deeper states even as a beginner.

Insight

However long the session, the benefits ripple out far beyond it, just as with the proverbial pebble dropped into water. Remember that meditation is not a competition. Every experience of meditation is slightly different. Don't set out with a goal and then consider the session a failure because you didn't achieve it. Just experience and enjoy whatever occurs.

Give yourself some cognitive self-therapy

Why are you stressed? Why aren't you relaxed? Okay, we all know what you're probably going to say. There's *this* problem. There's *that* problem. Somebody *said* something annoying. Somebody else *did* something annoying. Of *course* you're stressed.

But hang on a minute. Suppose I tell you you're only stressed about those things because you've *chosen* to be stressed about them. Suppose I say that what's made you annoyed is not the external event but you yourself. It's *your reaction* that's the problem.

Yes, I know it's hard to take in the concept at first. You're probably right now saying you've never read such nonsense. But just think about it for a moment. Let's say, for example, you've just received a telephone call at work from a customer making a complaint. You don't think the complaint is justified and, what's more, the customer is being rude and aggressive. You feel angry and your body begins to pump those stress hormones into your system. Five minutes ago you were perfectly happy and relaxed and now you're irritable and tense.

But why? If you're astonished by the question that just shows how much you've been conditioned to see anger as the correct reaction. Let's just analyse it. It's the customer who has the problem, not you. If the customer lacks manners then, once again, that's the customer problem, not yours. You're not going to get paid less money at the end of the month. Your anger and tension aren't going to achieve anything for you or anybody else. You're not being physically harmed in any way.

You won't suffer any mental harm, either, if you adopt the following attitude: Imagine you're a fish swimming in a river into which anglers have cast various baited hooks. If you swallow the bait you're lost. But you don't have to. You can keep on swimming and simply ignore those hooks.

The hooks, of course, represent all those things that are going to make you angry.

This is just one aspect of a whole way of looking at life that's known a cognitive therapy. It was developed as a tool to help psychotherapists treat depression, and it has been very successful. But it's just as useful for people in everyday life too. The essence of cognitive therapy is that it's your thoughts (cognitions) that create your feelings, much more so than the things that are happening to you. In other words, you can learn to be relaxed and unstressed in the midst of turmoil.

Insight

Let that idea sink in for a moment. Remember how as a kid another child might have said something hurtful and you replied with, 'Nuh ni nuh ni nuh nuh'. Instinctively you were trying to convince yourself it didn't hurt, probably with only partial success. But you were on the right lines.

Below is a summary of the faulty, negative thinking recognized by cognitive therapy, contrasted with the right, positive way of thinking.

BLACK-AND-WHITE

If you're not utterly successful you see yourself as a failure because you don't allow for all the shades of grey. So you're stressed.

But you could be thinking: 'I may not be top but I'm really pleased with what I've achieved.'

FOCUSING ON THE NEGATIVE

A hundred things are absolutely fine, but you can only think about the one thing that's wrong. You exaggerate its importance. Or, because one thing is wrong, you see it as part of a whole negative pattern. So you're stressed.

But you could be thinking: 'There are so many good things to be pleased about that I'm not even going to think about the one that's wrong.'

JUMPING TO NEGATIVE CONCLUSIONS

When you don't know what's happening (somebody is late, your boss hasn't yet told you the results of your annual review) you always assume the worst. So you're stressed.

But you could be thinking: 'I'll assume everything is fine until I hear otherwise.'

LABELLING

You attach labels to everyone, including yourself. One mistake and you're a 'moron'. So you're stressed.

But you could be thinking: 'There's a lot more to me, and everyone else, than a simplistic label.'

THINGS YOU SHOULD DO

You have preconceived ideas about the way you *should* behave. I *should* apply for a better job. I *should* be more successful. So you're stressed.

But you could be thinking: 'I'll only do what I feel happy and relaxed about.'

WRONGLY TAKING RESPONSIBILITY

You see yourself as personally responsible when other people don't behave as you think they should. So you're stressed.

But you could be thinking: 'Other people have to take responsibility for their own actions.'

This is a fairly complicated subject and we'll be looking at it again in the next chapter in the context of creating happiness. You might also like to have a look at the Taking it further section (page 260).

For now, just keep in mind that you *can* cut your stress levels, if you'll only stop torturing yourself with negative thoughts and replace them with positive ones.

Sleep

When it comes to sleep and longevity there are two very different, contradictory theories. There's what might be called the 'Sleeping Beauty' theory. And there's what might be called the 'New York' theory.

The 'Sleeping Beauty' theory goes like this. The more you sleep the more beautiful – or, at least, more youthful – you'll remain. Why? Because when you sleep *without dreaming* your heart rate, breathing, kidney function, muscle tension, movement and ultimately temperature (which reaches its lowest point around 5 a.m.) are at their absolute minimum. And if you remember your Metabolic Theory (page 130), the more energy you conserve the longer you live.

And we all know we just feel better when we have a good night's sleep. When we don't, we may feel irritable, lethargic and unable to concentrate. That much has been proven in various experiments. Researchers at London's Westminster University discovered that 7.20 a.m. was the magic cut-off. People who got up before 7.20 a.m. had raised levels of the stress hormone cortisol compared with people who got up after 7.20 a.m., *irrespective of the time they went to bed.*

Moreover, sleep is associated with higher levels of melatonin, a hormone that:

- ▶ *boosts the immune system*
- ▶ *is a powerful antioxidant (see Chapters 2 and 3)*
- ▶ *seems to prolong life.*

In fact, mice given melatonin lived 20 to 30 per cent longer than mice in a control group without extra melatonin. So, the message seems obvious. Sleep 12 hours a day and live to be 120.

But not so fast! Because the 'New York' theory – named after the city that never sleeps – says precisely the opposite. Proof for that comes from the biggest ever sleep study which found that the optimum amount of sleep for longevity was precisely seven hours. Not six, not eight and certainly not 12.

It's a study that has to be taken seriously. It was so large and so detailed that it took more than a decade to analyse the data. A team at the University of California, San Diego School of Medicine in collaboration with the American Cancer Society tracked more than one million adults aged between 30 and 102 for six years. Moreover, the researchers were able to match individuals with similar profiles in terms of age, diet, exercise, smoking, previous health problems and so on. So none of that affected the findings. Within the six year period, 5.1 per cent of the women and 9.4 per cent of the men died. From analysing the sleep patterns of those who lived and those who died the scientists concluded that seven hours was the optimum for longevity for both men and women. Those sleeping eight hours, for example, were 12 per cent more likely to die, other factors being equal.

When people slept either less or more than seven hours, mortality increased. And here's the interesting thing. It's more dangerous to sleep longer than to sleep less. At ten hours or more, for example, the risk is enormous. Far worse, even, than sleeping three hours. Intriguingly, the average amount of sleep in the Western world has fallen from nine hours a century ago to around seven-and-a-half hours now – a period that's seen a steady rise in longevity.

What can we make of all this? One thing that's clear from the San Diego findings is that those people who believe they have sleep problems may not have a problem at all. Getting just five hours' sleep a night is better, in terms of longevity, than getting eight. It sounds counterintuitive but it's what the statistics tell us. Why should it be? Even the man who led the research, Daniel F. Kripke M.D., is baffled. It could simply be that spending a long time asleep allows everything to, as it were, 'clog up'. More research is needed.

So what should you do? Sleep more or sleep less? Until we have further data the best policy would seem to be to back both horses. *Sleep* seven hours but *relax* in bed a while longer. For example, get up and make a cup of tea and then return to bed to drink it.

Older people tend to have more problems with sleep than younger people. If this is true for you, the conclusion of this study is clear – just don't worry about it. If you're getting five hours a night that's absolutely fine from the point of view of your health. But if you'd like to get your optimum seven hours and can't, here are some tips:

▶ *Always discuss things that bother you. Don't repress them, because they can manifest themselves as nightmares.*
▶ *Set a cut-off time for problem-solving. Say 8 p.m. If any problems are left over, write them down in your diary for tomorrow and forget about them.*
▶ *Make time to relax and unwind before going to bed; keep the lights low and don't watch or read anything disturbing.*
▶ *Make sure your bedroom is quiet, dark and warm and that your bed is comfortable.*
▶ *Get enough mental and physical exercise during the day so that you feel mentally and physically tired by bedtime.*
▶ *Don't eat your last meal too late and make it light but with plenty of carbohydrates such as beans, pasta or bananas (because they contain tryptophan, an amino acid conducive to sleep).*
▶ *Limit your alcohol intake in the evening, because it's disturbing to deep sleep.*
▶ *Avoid caffeine, chocolate and spicy foods in the evening.*
▶ *Practise meditation and cognitive self-therapy to keep those night-time worries at bay.*
▶ *After getting into bed, do the muscular relaxation exercise opposite.*

Insight

Your sleep follows a 90-minute cycle, oscillating between deep sleep and lighter sleep with dreams. These dreaming periods are accompanied by rapid eye movement and are therefore called REM sleep. Heart and breathing rates go up, especially if the dream is a frightening one, so you're not saving energy when you're dreaming. Most sleep researchers have assumed that dreaming is important and Freud believed it was one of the whole points of sleeping, by dissipating excess sexual tension, anxiety and excitement. But a psychiatrist called George Vogel discovered he could completely deprive people of REM sleep for three weeks (by waking them whenever he detected the rapid eye movements) without any ill effects. In fact, waking people during the REM phase has been successfully used to treat depression. So maybe dreaming isn't essential after all.

Muscular relaxation

When your muscles are relaxed your mind is relaxed. Here's a little 16-step exercise you can practise during the day or when you go to bed. If you hold each muscle contraction for about ten seconds, followed by about ten seconds of relaxation, you can complete the whole process in under ten minutes. But you can also do it more quickly or more slowly and repeat it as much as necessary.

Lie down flat on the floor or in bed, with your arms by your sides, palms uppermost and feet roughly shoulder-width apart. Then:

1 *Curl the toes of both feet towards the soles. Hold. Relax.*
2 *Curl the toes of both feet away from the soles. Hold. Relax.*
3 *Press the backs of your knees against the floor/bed. Hold. Relax.*
4 *Turn your toes inwards towards each other. Hold. Relax.*
5 *Pull your abdomen in towards your tensed buttocks while exhaling. Hold. Relax.*
6 *Pull your navel back towards your spine while exhaling. Hold. Relax.*
7 *Expand your ribs to the maximum while inhaling. Hold. Relax.*

8   *Press the small of your back against the floor/bed. Hold. Relax.*
9   *Make fists as tight as you can. Hold. Relax.*
10 *Press your wrists, palms up, against the floor/bed. Hold. Relax.*
11 *Press your elbows against the floor/bed. Hold. Relax.*
12 *Press your chin against your chest. Hold. Relax.*
13 *Press the back of your head against the floor/bed. Hold. Relax.*
14 *Press your tongue against the roof of your mouth (lips together). Hold. Relax.*
15 *Squeeze your eyes tightly shut. Hold. Relax.*
16 *Imagine your brain floating weightlessly inside your skull. Relax.*

Laughter – the stress-breaker

If you think you should only smile and laugh when you're happy and relaxed then think again, because you can smile and laugh to make yourself happy and relaxed. Or as William James, the psychologist brother of novelist Henry, put it: 'We don't laugh because we're happy, we are happy because we laugh.'

If it sounds crazy to smile and laugh for no reason, it's even crazier not to. Here's the evidence. Smiles and laughter:

▶ *lower stress hormones, including cortisol*
▶ *lower blood pressure (after an initial increase)*
▶ *increase the disease-fighting protein gamma-interferon*
▶ *increase T cells and B cells which make disease-fighting antibodies*
▶ *increase Immunoglobulin A, the body's first line of defence against infections of the upper respiratory tract*
▶ *increase Immunoglobulins M and G*
▶ *increase Complement 3, which helps antibodies pierce defective or infected cells in order to destroy them*

- ▶ *benefit anyone suffering from diabetes because laughter lowers blood sugar*
- ▶ *benefit the heart*
- ▶ *strengthen abdominal muscles*
- ▶ *relax the body*
- ▶ *reduce pain, possibly by the production of endorphins but certainly through relaxation and distraction*
- ▶ *flush water vapour from the lungs*
- ▶ *speed recovery from surgery, especially for children. One extra reason to laugh...*
- ▶ *It stops everyone from thinking you're dull.*

But how can you smile for no reason? Easy! Just turn up the corners of your mouth and do it. That simple muscular movement sets in motion chemical changes that are good for you. It's been proven. As regards laughing, you must have noticed how you and everybody else sometimes laugh at a very tense or awkward moment. You can see it at the cinema. Something terrible seems to be about to happen... but then it doesn't... and everybody laughs. It doesn't have to be funny. It's an instinctive way of dispelling the tension. And you can use it in everyday life. When you don't agree with someone, don't get aggressive. Instead, try to find a way of putting across your point of view with a smile and then a laugh. (Not at the other person, of course.) You'll find it works much better and keeps everyone's stress levels down.

TRY THIS

One researcher has concluded that adults in the West laugh an average of just 17 times a day. That's not actually very much. Little more than once an hour, in fact. Aim to at least treble that.

Every time you laugh today make a quick note of it somewhere handy. In fact, the back of your hand could be the very place. Just make a little mark with a pen. At the end of the day, tot up the number of marks. If it isn't over 40 you've got some homework to do.

Close your eyes and think of something funny that happened recently. Replay it in your mind. If you can't think of anything from real life replay a scene from a movie. Let yourself smile. Then let yourself chuckle. Then let yourself laugh. If you're with someone else, share the scenario with them.

Insight

If you're in pain you may be able to use laughter in a very specific way. Do something to increase the pain. Yes, increase it. If it's an arthritic joint, for example, move it. If it's an injury, press it. Then laugh. Keep on doing it. Pain. Laugh. Pain. Laugh. Pain. Laugh. After a while, you won't feel the pain so much.

Warning – laughing can sometimes be a bad thing

There are just a few medical conditions that could be made worse by too much laughing. If you're asthmatic, laughing just might trigger an attack. It can also be bad for anyone with a serious heart condition, a hernia, severe piles, certain eye problems, and anyone who has just undergone abdominal surgery.

10 THINGS TO REMEMBER

1 *According to Metabolic Theory, the less energy you burn the longer you live – so relax.*

2 *Take a lesson from the Slow Movement and learn to savour everything you do, from eating to sightseeing.*

3 *Eustress, the kind of stress you experience when you enjoy a challenge, can be stimulating, but chronic distress, by contrast, can cause serious health problems.*

4 *Avoid situations you find highly stressful and, at the same time, increase your ability to cope with stress.*

5 *Downsizing is one possible way of lowering stress.*

6 *Meditation is proven to be successful at increasing stress resistance.*

7 *Cognitive self-therapy is an effective way of overcoming anxiety and feeling more relaxed.*

8 *The optimum number of hours of sleep for longevity seems to be seven.*

9 *A simple muscle-relaxing technique can also help you relax your mind.*

10 *Use smiles and laughter as a way of dispelling tension.*

HOW MUCH LONGER ARE YOU GOING TO LIVE NOW?

▶ *When you're not exercising are you taking things slowly?*
▶ *Are you improving your ability to deal with the stressful situations you can't avoid, and avoiding the stressful situations you can't deal with?*
▶ *Are you giving serious consideration to downsizing?*
▶ *Are you meditating regularly?*
▶ *Are you giving yourself cognitive therapy so as to avoid anger, negativity and guilt?*
▶ *Have you set an evening cut-off time for dealing with problems, or even thinking about them?*
▶ *Are you sleeping seven hours or less a night but relaxing in bed for a while before getting up?*
▶ *Are you practising muscular relaxation, especially after getting into bed?*
▶ *Have you been laughing for no 'good' reason?*
▶ *Have you tried laughter for pain relief and stress-breaking?*

Score:

If you answered 'yes' to seven or more questions you're obviously a natural at relaxing. If you also exercise as described in Chapter 4 then the two things combined will significantly increase your life expectancy. Move on to the next chapter.

If you answered 'yes' to between four and six questions you're well on the way to developing the right frame of mind for a tranquil and long life but you should endeavour (gently) to do a bit more. You can also move on to the next chapter but re-read this one from time to time and try to follow further recommendations.

If you answered 'yes' to three or fewer questions you undoubtedly have a big problem relaxing. You're probably the kind of person who thinks it necessary to confront anything you don't like or don't agree with. For the sake of enjoying a longer life you need to think carefully about the issues raised in this chapter. Read it again and aim to get your score up to a least four before moving on.

7

....

Happiness

In this chapter you will learn:
- *why happy people live longer*
- *how negative thoughts and negative emotions can make you ill*
- *that happiness is something that can be learned.*

Happy people live longer. It's that simple. And, fortunately for the vast majority of us, happiness is a state of mind that can be learned. Contrary to popular belief, you don't have to be rich, famous or beautiful to be happy. Being born with the right genes helps. But genes are only part of the story. How happy you feel right now is largely down to things that are within your control.

The good news on ageing is that older people *tend* to be happier than younger people. And the myth of the grumpy old man is just that, a myth. There are plenty of grumpy *middle-aged* men, though. The curious fact is that the steady increase in men's happiness over the years suddenly dives between the ages of 45 and 54 and doesn't turn upwards again until between the ages of 55 and 64. After which, men become happier than ever. For women there's good news and bad news. On average they're more contented than men until well into their sixties. But thereafter only a quarter of women as opposed to half of men (in one survey, anyway) describe themselves as 'very happy'. They obviously have other things going for them in terms of longevity.

One of the most reliable ways to become happier is simply to *deliberately think happy thoughts*. It sounds too easy to be true. But it is true. And science has proven it quite convincingly. Happiness is very much a matter of the way you perceive the world.

Every day there are good and bad things happening. You can *choose* to be happy about the good things or you can *choose* to be miserable about the bad things. It's up to you.

Be grateful

Let's start with you. What are your good points? Write them down. You don't have to be 'world class' in any of them to add them to your list. Here are some suggestions to get you going:

- *I don't deliberately harm anybody else.*
- *I always make time for my friends when they have problems.*
- *I'm quite good at telling jokes and making people laugh.*
- *I don't make a fuss when things go wrong.*
- *I'm good at drawing.*
- *Dogs like me.*

Now you make your own list.

Insight

If you really can't think of anything then you're being too hard on yourself. In fact, if your sheet of paper is blank or has only a couple of points written on it then we don't have to look very far for one of the sources of your unhappiness. You don't like yourself enough. You don't love yourself enough. Well, you should. For a start, you're certainly modest. So put that down. You're obviously sensitive. So put that down. You're also introspective. Add that to the list. That's three useful qualities already.

Many unhappy people simply demand too much of themselves, and those around them, too. We're all human beings – animals, in fact – with enormous limitations. You're going to have to learn to accept that about yourself and your fellow man and woman. Just do your best. Nobody can ask more.

Now get back to the list and don't stop until you've got at least 20 things written down.

When you've finished writing about yourself, make a list of all the good points about your partner. Again, here are some suggestions to get you going:

- ▶ *He/she seldom gets angry.*
- ▶ *He/she never spends money without discussing it with me first.*
- ▶ *He/she is always very considerate towards my parents.*
- ▶ *He/she looks after me when I'm ill.*
- ▶ *He/she likes many of the same things I do.*
- ▶ *He/she makes me laugh.*
- ▶ *He/she cooks beautiful meals for me.*

And then do the same for your children, your parents and anyone else you're close to.

Insight
If you really can't think of anything then it's not just a question of being too hard on the people around you. There's obviously some kind of deep resentment at work, because everybody has good qualities even if they have a few bad ones, too, and you're going to have to discharge that resentment. We'll be taking a deeper look at your relationships in Chapter 9.

Now you're going to make a list of all the good things in your life. For example:

- ▶ *I'm in good health.*
- ▶ *I have somewhere nice to live.*

- *I never have to go hungry.*
- *I have many friends.*

Now make your list. Begin with your body. If it works pretty much as it should then that's already something to be very happy about. Can you see? Can you hear? Can you touch things? Can you taste things? Can you smell them? Can you remember things? Can you run? Can you swim? Can you make love? This is going to be a pretty long list.

Insight

Nobody's list should – could – be short. If yours is then you've got to learn to appreciate things more than you do. You're taking far too much for granted. You've got to learn to stop comparing with the ultimate – the richest person, the biggest house, the strongest athlete – and try to get a bit more perspective. Don't forget there are also people who have almost nothing to eat, who don't have any kind of house and who combat severe disabilities.

When you've finished your lists copy them out very clearly onto some card or, if you have a computer, print them. Also make the 'highlights' into a portable version you can keep in your wallet or handbag. Make sure you always have copies close to hand. Here's what you do.

- *When you get up in the morning read the lists.*
- *When you're having lunch read the lists.*
- *Just before you go to sleep read the lists.*
- *Any time you're feeling unhappy or cross with your partner or people close to you read the lists.*

Insight

That probably sounds a rather silly idea and you may already have made up your mind not to do it. Well, it's been *proven* to work. In fact, it's an extremely powerful technique for achieving happiness. So try it.

Getting rid of negative thoughts

So far in this chapter we've talked about taking stock of all the good things in your life – things you should be happy and grateful about. Well, it's a process you can, and should, take much further. Essentially, you can build a happy brain, because as we saw in Chapter 5, your brain is plastic.

In other words, it can be moulded. In effect, the same way as a muscle can. And not just when you're an infant. All through your life your brain has the capacity for physical change. Only a very few functions are irrevocably set in childhood. So, it doesn't matter how old you are now, you still have the possibility of becoming profoundly happy and lengthening your life as a result.

Neurologists have a saying: 'Cells that fire together wire together.' It's one of the answers to the riddle of how the brain works. When two things happen at once, such as seeing the sun and feeling delicious warmth on your skin, two sets of neurons are set off in your brain and a connection, known as a synapse, is made between them. You've now learned that sunshine means pleasure. And forever more, when you see the sun, you'll feel happy. What's more, each time you feel the pleasure, the synapse will be strengthened. This is called Hebbian Learning, after the Canadian psychologist Donald Hebb who, as far back as 1949, proposed that single neurons were responsible for the learning process.

We can use this knowledge to help us 'rip out' the 'negative' wiring and replace it with 'positive' wiring. The concept is profound and yet very simple. If you deliberately stop thinking negative thoughts in connection with certain events and, instead, think positive thoughts, then *the chemicals that are linked to your thoughts will bring about physical changes in your brain.*

This idea that happiness comes from controlling your own mind rather than the outside world has long been a teaching of Oriental philosophy. But, relatively recently, it's also become a teaching of modern psychology. In the 1960s Dr Aaron Beck at the University of Pennsylvania School of Medicine began codifying the different kinds of thinking that lead to happiness and unhappiness. As a result he developed a system for treating depression and various other mental problems which he called 'cognitive therapy'.

Let's say you're made redundant. These are two possible responses:

1 *I'm a failure; I'll never get another job now.*
2 *What a fantastic opportunity! I was really getting into a rut and now I have the chance to do something different.*

Obviously, if you were to give response (1), you'd be talking yourself into a depression and building a depressed brain. But if you were to give response (2) you'd be much happier – and, incidentally, far more likely to get another job.

This more positive way of looking at the world is the essence of cognitive therapy (CT). Some people object to CT on the grounds that it implies problems aren't real but are 'all in the mind'. That's a misunderstanding of CT. Of course CT recognizes that the situation is real. The facts are the facts. But you may be perceiving them in a far more negative way than you need.

Here are some of the negative 'traps'.

IF IT'S NOT BLACK IT MUST BE WHITE

This is a style of thinking that helps to keep life simple and, indeed, there's also a kind of security in it. But it makes no allowance for reality, which is that between black and white there are infinite shades of grey. Consequently, people who limit themselves to thinking this way tend to miss out on a lot and suffer a good deal of unnecessary misery. If you're a 'black-and-whiter' then either you're a success or you're a failure. Either you're attractive or you're ugly. Either you're a great raconteur or you're a bore. And since nobody is in the top drawer in every category, anyone with this outlook is going to feel despondent a lot of the time.

Try this

Think of something at which you've always considered yourself a complete failure, completely *black* (I'm hopeless at my job/conversation/attracting the opposite sex). Then write down the following things:

▶ *The amount of training you've received to do that thing.*
▶ *The amount of effort you've made.*
▶ *Any examples of where you came somewhere between failure and success.*

Ask yourself this: Is it really all black, or is it a shade of grey?

IF IT'S NOT PERFECT IT'S NO GOOD

Perfectionism is something different from being conscientious, meticulous and painstaking. It's striving for a level so unrealistically high that you're either so intimidated you can't even begin or you can't ever finish. That's no use to anybody. You just make yourself unhappy along with everybody else you're involved with.

You may believe, as so many do, that perfection does exist. But I'm going to prove to you that in terms of the things human beings do, it doesn't. Oh, okay, if I ask you two plus two and you answer four then, yes, that's the perfect answer. But let's look at things that are a little more complicated.

The test is this. If something is perfect it's incapable of improvement. So let's take a look around. Your TV? Is the picture quality so good it could never be improved? Obviously not. Could your car be more durable, quieter, more fuel efficient? Obviously it could. Have you ever seen a film in which every line of dialogue was convincing, every gesture accurate, every camera angle satisfying and the plot always clear? No. I won't go on. When you think about it you'll see that perfection of that kind doesn't exist.

Try this

1 *Whatever you have to do today, set out to do it to a good and competent standard but not to perfection. At the end of the*

day work out how much you got through compared with a
'perfectionist day'.

2   Take a look at yourself in the mirror. Too short at 5' 2"?
   Who says? In fact, you're a perfect example of a person of
   5' 2". Too many freckles? Who says? In fact, you're a perfect
   example of freckles. Bald? You're a perfect example of
   baldness. So now go out in the garden and learn to see that
   everything there is a perfect and unique example of itself –
   each flower different, each flower perfect.

WHY IS THIS ALWAYS HAPPENING TO ME?

Most of us focus far too much on the negative and, what's more,
exaggerate the significance of anything that goes wrong. The whole
thing is summed up in that well-known phrase: Why is this *always*
happening to me?

We get angry and allow our emotions to build and cloud our
judgement.

You know the kind of thing. You get a bird-dropping on your
clothes and you say it. You get a puncture and you say it. You get
a parking ticket and you say it. And yet it's *never* true. You get a
parking ticket once a year, a bird-dropping on your clothes once in
five years and a puncture once a decade.

What makes you notice these things is not that they *always* happen
but that they happen so *seldom*. In fact, if they *always* happened
you wouldn't bother to mention the subject.

Try this
Every time you find yourself exaggerating a problem or a fault,
stop! Instead, look for the positive. It will be there.

I'M NOT GOING TO LIKE THIS

Your partner is late. You look at your watch and begin to get
angry. A little while later your anger starts to become overlaid

with concern. 'He's had an accident.' 'She's been abducted.' You're worried and very unhappy.

After an hour your partner arrives. What happened? It turns out to have been nothing more than a simple misunderstanding over the time. One of you thought you'd agreed on 8 o'clock, the other 9 o'clock. Or something like that.

These kinds of situations happen. The people whispering in the corner, who – you convince yourself – are saying bad things about you. The boss who doesn't greet you in the usual, cheerful way because – you convince yourself – he's about to reprimand you. The medical test which – you convince yourself – is bound to have found a life-threatening condition.

In the same vein, we all also like to have a go at predicting the future and enjoy saying 'I told you so' when our forecasts turn out to be right. And the predictions are usually negative. But we tend to forget the occasions when we were wrong. If you're someone who always has a negative view of things you may be surprised how many times that happens. Let's find out.

Try this
Carry a notebook with you for the next week. Every time a negative prediction comes into your mind, write it down. Things like:

- ▸ *I'm never going to be able to do this.*
- ▸ *He's going to cause trouble for me.*
- ▸ *She isn't going to like me.*
- ▸ *They look very suspicious.*
- ▸ *There's no way out of this.*
- ▸ *It can only mean something terrible has happened.*

When the outcome of the situation is known, write it in your notebook. At the end of the week, tot up how many times your negative predictions turned out to be right and how many wrong. You'll almost certainly find the latter outweigh the former by a considerable margin.

I FEEL IT SO IT MUST BE TRUE

The ugly duckling that becomes a swan is a story that goes back as long as stories have been told. The duckling *feels* ugly (usually because of things others have said) and comes to believe it must be true. And so it can be with many other emotions. For example, you've reached the big six zero so you *feel* you're getting old and you start to act it. You *feel* nobody likes you and conclude that you're unlovable. You *feel* you can't cope and conclude you're a bad grandparent. But your feelings can be wrong. For sure, you're far more of a swan than you realize.

Try this
Next time you feel the kinds of emotions that undermine your self-esteem, write them down. Then try to analyse the situation objectively. If you can't, enlist the help of a friend. Write down six reasons why your emotion wasn't justified.

I'M A LABEL, YOU'RE A LABEL

As with the black-and-white approach, labels can make life simpler. I'm a loser. He's a moron. She's a thicko. They're unbeatable. Once the label has been decided, there's no need to look any more deeply or keep the situation under review. And that's exactly why labelling is a disaster. It's far too simplistic, takes no account of change and, worst of all, is self-fulfilling.

For example, when you go to play the tennis partners who are 'unbeatable' you'll have given up before even hitting the first ball. When you decide you're a 'loser' you won't even try any more. And when you treat other people as 'idiots' you don't give them the opportunity to tackle problems and grow.

Try this
1   *Write down the names of all the people to whom you've attributed labels. Include yourself, if you've given yourself a label. Next to the names write the label. Now, in each case, find six reasons why the label is inappropriate.*

2   *Choose a subject at which you've labelled yourself a failure
and given up trying (I can't dance/play tennis/do maths
or whatever). Then take lessons from a properly qualified
teacher. You may not be the best but you'll discover that
you're certainly not a 'failure' either.*

I SHOULD DO THIS, YOU SHOULD DO THAT

We all have a little voice within telling us what we *should* do.
(And quite often it's reinforced by someone else's voice, too.)
I *should* cut the grass, even though it's only an inch long. I *should*
clean the house, even though I did it last week. I *should* go to Bill
and Sheila's party, even though we have nothing in common. And
when you don't do what you *should*, you feel guilt.

Maybe you also direct 'should' statements at others. You *should*
smarten yourself up a bit. You *should* go to the funeral. You
should get a better job. If the people you're directing the statements
at don't take any notice you end up feeling frustrated and resentful.

Try this
For the next week banish all 'shoulds' and see what happens.
Each time you're faced with a 'should situation' apply a different
mindset to it: *Taking all things into account, will I be happier if
I do this or if I don't?*

As regards other people, ask yourself this: *What right have I got to
tell someone else what to do?*

IF IT'S WRONG IT MUST BE MY FAULT

Accepting responsibility for things that aren't your responsibility
is a common error, particularly among women. Women are the
nurturing sex so it's understandable that they react this way more
often than men do.

Let's say that your elderly father insists on driving. He hasn't had
an accident yet but you're convinced it's only a matter of time – and

not very much time. You feel it's your responsibility to tell him to sell the car. You lay awake at night worrying about how to persuade him – and how he'll manage without it. You're unhappy.

But let's look at the facts. Your father is an adult, with more experience than you have, and makes his own decisions. He hasn't had an accident, which probably means he's acknowledged his limitations and drives accordingly. The police haven't interfered. His doctor hasn't interfered. So why should you?

Try this
Make a checklist of 25 things involving other people that you consider yourself to be responsible for (for example, ironing his shirts, checking that your partner is 'correctly' dressed, making sure the kids do their homework). Then go through the list asking yourself:

- ▶ *Am I really responsible for this?*
- ▶ *Why can't the other person do this for him/herself?*
- ▶ *In what way am I so superior that only I can do this?*
- ▶ *In what way is the other person so inferior as to be incapable of doing this?*

How negative emotions can poison you

When you think in a negative way you have negative emotions, and they can literally poison you. Anger is an excellent example. Anger is the way to escalate a situation, both internally and externally. **The idea that you can get rid of your anger by letting it out is completely wrong.** Shouting at somebody, or shouting at an empty chair which represents somebody, or punching pillows is the exact opposite of what's needed.

The best way to counter anger (and all the other negative emotions) is to understand the other person's position. In other words, to empathize. By all means discuss why you feel angry – that's always a good idea – but it's completely different from venting your anger as if it's steam escaping from a pressure cooker. **What you actually need to do is turn off the heat.**

Insight

From what you now know about the workings of your brain you can see the danger. When you allow your anger to build up, you're actually strengthening the 'anger synapses' in your brain. You're moulding your brain for anger. Far from getting rid of the anger you're redesigning the capacity of your brain to create more anger. It's a disaster. Don't make the mistake of thinking that empathy is primarily for the benefit of another person: empathy is for your benefit.

Try this

For the next week, do your best to empathize with everyone you're in contact with, especially anyone with whom you're in conflict. When someone is angry with you, do your best not to get angry back.

Before you ask any questions out loud try to imagine *why* they're behaving as they are. Don't label them as, say, troublemakers or neurotics; *don't* try to reduce the situation to an issue of black and white, look for the grey. Start from the position that the other person is a perfectly reasonable human being (normally a correct assumption) and must have a valid reason for their behaviour.

Now, in a calm tone of voice, ask questions. How do you see the situation? What would you like to do about it? What is it that's making you angry? Why are you so upset about this?

When the other person replies, *don't* focus on the things you disagree with. Instead, do your very best to **find something to agree with**.

When you do that, you'll defuse the other person's anger as well as your own. Then, with both of you in a more positive frame of mind, you can start to sort out the areas of disagreement. And hopefully come to a *happy* conclusion.

How negative emotions are dangerous for your health

A link between emotion and illness has long been postulated but it was only in the 1970s that a psychologist called Robert Ader uncovered one of the mechanisms. He gave rats saccharin-flavoured water along with a chemical that suppressed T-cells. Later he gave just the saccharin-flavoured water but the rats' T-cell count still went down. The significance of the experiment was that it proved a connection between the brain (which 'tasted' the water) and the immune system.

Soon afterwards, a colleague at the University of Rochester School of Medicine and Dentistry, David Felten, pinpointed synapse-like contacts where the autonomic nervous system (responsible for 'running' the body) spoke to the immune cells using neurotransmitters.

There's at least one other mechanism connecting emotions and physical health. During stress, the body releases a cocktail of hormones including adrenaline (epinephrine), noradrenaline (norepinephrine), cortisol and prolactin. Generally speaking, these 'stress hormones' have the effect of suppressing the immune system. Why evolution should have arranged things that way can only be conjectured. Possibly it's a method of conserving energy during an emergency.

The problem is that if stress is prolonged or constant (if, for example, you nurture your negative emotions) then your immune system will be permanently compromised.

What's more, stress hormones lead to higher levels of glucose, cholesterol and fat in the blood to provide the energy for physical action. But if physical action doesn't follow,

plaque gets deposited on the walls of the blood vessels.
To that long-term risk can be added the short-term risk of a
heart attack when noradrenaline levels are sharply elevated.

A list of the disorders related to negative emotion includes:
allergies, asthma, cancers, colds and flu, depression,
diabetes, headaches, heart disease, hypertension, indigestion,
muscle pain and cramps, sexual problems, strokes and
ulcers.

The conclusion is simple: Be happy, stay healthy, live
longer.

Applying the lessons to your past

In the words of the song, you've got regrets. But are they too few
to mention? Or do they bother you? If they do, you can apply the
same principles of cognitive therapy to them.

But surely, you say, we can't change our past lives? Surely we can't
change the facts of history? Well, no, we can't change the facts but
are you sure they are the facts? We only remember a tiny fraction of
past events and, to some extent, we *choose* our memories to fit with
the world view we've selected for ourselves. Some people choose to
remember the best and some choose to remember the worst.

Are you, for example, one of the many people who have been
through a separation or divorce? What, then, are your memories
of your ex-partner? Can you remember that you once loved him
or her? Or can you only recall the rows and the flying saucepans?
Do you only want to remember the rows and the flying saucepans?
That's most likely the case. But there *was* a time when you were in
love. There *was* a time when you were happy together. Why not
remember *those* times?

It doesn't mean pretending the bad things never happened. You may, indeed, have to face up to those bad things and deal with them. But it may be that you have feelings of bitterness and resentment, which are spoiling your present life, and that actually aren't justified.

Try this
Every day find a quiet time to mull over your past. When you go to bed can be a good moment. Re-examine those events you think of as negative and that bother you. Ask yourself these questions:

▶ *Were they really as uniformly* black *as I've painted them; wasn't there maybe a little grey, too, or even white?*
▶ *Am I applying standards that would have required* perfection *on the part of myself or others?*
▶ *Am I* exaggerating *the negative?*
▶ *Am I applying glib labels with the benefit of hindsight?*
▶ *Is it really the case that I, or others, should have behaved differently?*
▶ *Am I* wrongly taking responsibility *for things?*

Sometimes events bother us more in retrospect than they did at the time. Also ask yourself this: Am I seeing the past through my eyes now or my eyes then?

Insight
Neuro-Linguistic Programming (NLP) has some special techniques for dealing with unpleasant memories from the past. One is to stop revisiting the memory vividly as if it has only just happened. Instead, give the memory the qualities ('submodalities' in NLP jargon) of a very ancient memory (colours faded to pale sepia, jerky 'Charlie Chaplin' movements, faint crackly voices...) and push it to the far end of your 'timeline' of past events, as if, instead, it happened a century ago.

Enough money for a happy future?

As we get older many of us become preoccupied with having enough money for retirement. But does money buy happiness? Well, there's no doubt that an inability to pay the bills causes *un*happiness. There's no doubt that having an insufficient pension for a few of life's little pleasures causes *un*happiness.

But beyond that, there's not much evidence of a strong positive effect of wealth on happiness. A person who earns £1 million a year isn't ten times happier than a person earning £100,000. Nor even twice as happy. Maybe, at a pinch, 10 per cent more happy. Maybe not at all.

A survey in Britain found that 60 per cent of those in the top social classes ABC1 felt 'very pleased with things yesterday, all or most of the time' compared with 55 per cent for DEs. That's a small difference easily explained by the fact that DEs tend to suffer the negative effects of financial hardship. In fact, in that particular survey, C2s were the happiest at 62 per cent.

A survey in America found that the very rich (incomes of over $10 million a year) were happy 77 per cent of the time compared with 62 per cent for controls chosen at random from the same area. That's a more significant difference but, again, some of the controls would have faced financial problems.

Several studies have shown that when people win large sums of money they don't become happier in the medium to longer term. Nor are people generally happier in wealthier countries compared with poorer countries. Nor does an increase in national wealth result in more happiness. Americans seem to be no happier now than they were in 1946/7, in the cheerful optimism after the end of the Second World War, and are considerably *less* happy than they were in the late 1950s.

Try this

1 *Keep a Happiness Diary. That's to say, record when you feel happy and why. Review it from time to time to see where most of your happiness comes from. Is it from material possessions or life's inexpensive pleasures?*

2 *This month, don't buy anything other than necessities and don't use any expensive products (except where you have no alternative). Concentrate on finding happiness in things that are free or inexpensive, such as love, sex, friendship, pets, nature, swimming in the sea or a lake, walking or running, and identifying the stars.*

3 *Stop comparing with what other people have. Let me ask you this. Are you happier when you listen to music on an MP3 player than when you listen to the same music on a CD player? And did the music on the CD player make you happier in turn than the tape cassette? And did the cassette make you happier than listening at $33 \frac{1}{3}$ rpm? Of course not. It's the music that counts. In other words, what does it matter that someone has the latest media centre and you haven't? For the next month:*
   ▷ *don't look at any advertising*
   ▷ *don't go window shopping*
   ▷ *don't read any magazines depicting celebrities*
   ▷ *don't compare with the Joneses.*

10 THINGS TO REMEMBER

1 *Be grateful: make a list of all the good points about yourself, your life and everyone around you, and read it every day.*

2 *Your brain is plastic, which means it can be rebuilt as a 'happy brain' by thinking happy thoughts and by ridding yourself of negative thoughts (negative emotions can make you ill – be happy, stay healthy, live longer).*

3 *Cognitive therapy (CT) teaches that real life is shades of grey, not black and white, that it's futile aiming for perfection, that negative thoughts are inevitably exaggerated, that you shouldn't attach negative labels to yourself or others, and that predictions of disaster seldom come true.*

4 *You don't have to do what you should so much as what makes you happy, and you don't have to take responsibility for things that aren't your responsibility.*

5 *When you give in to anger you build an 'angry brain'.*

6 *The principal antidote to negative emotions about others is empathy.*

7 *Always start with the attitude that other people are reasonable and must have a valid reason for their behaviour.*

8 *Do your best to find things to agree with, not to disagree with.*

9 *Once you've learned to eliminate negative thoughts, apply the same process to your past.*

10 *Wealth has little to do with happiness.*

HOW MUCH LONGER ARE YOU GOING TO LIVE NOW?

▶ *Are you deliberately thinking happy thoughts?*
▶ *Have you made a list of all the good things about yourself, those close to you, and your life?*
▶ *Are you reading your list of 'good things' regularly?*
▶ *Are you ridding yourself of negative thoughts?*
▶ *Are you ridding yourself of negative emotions?*
▶ *Are you trying hard to empathize with other people?*
▶ *Have you rewritten the story of your life, focusing on the positive and happy parts?*
▶ *Have you started a Happiness Diary?*
▶ *Have you stopped comparing yourself with the wealthiest people?*
▶ *Have you accepted that you don't have to be rich to be happy?*

Score:

If you answered 'yes' to seven or more questions you're obviously a happy person and that, research shows, is very good for longevity. Move on to the next chapter.

If you answered 'yes' to between four and six questions you're well on the way to developing the right frame of mind for a happy and long life. You can also move on to the next chapter but re-read this one from time to time and be sure to practise the various exercises regularly.

If you answered 'yes' to three or fewer questions then, unless you've been blessed with 'happiness genes', you're probably not a very happy person. The good news is that happiness can be created quite deliberately. Once you accept that, you'll be better able to take control of your moods. Give the various exercises in this chapter a fair chance to work and, once you've reached at least four 'yesses' you can move on to the next chapter – but never stop doing the exercises.

8

Prudence

In this chapter you will learn:
- *steps you can take to reduce your risk of cancer*
- *the safe alcohol consumption limit for living longer*
- *what is the optimum amount of sunshine*
- *which medical checks are worth having.*

In the search for a longer life it's all too easy to overlook the obvious. Living longer isn't a question of discovering the mythical fountain of youth. It's to do with a whole range of lifestyle issues and some of them are very simple, even banal, everyday practices. They could be summed up with one word 'prudence'. It may not sound very exciting or glamorous, but prudence will get you a long way.

Some of the biggest differences between people who live to a great age and those who die much younger are actually to do with very commonplace things. For instance: whether or not you smoke, the amount of alcohol you drink, how you drive, or the frequency of your medical check-ups. These are all things that can have an impact on your life expectancy – in some cases a very dramatic impact.

Avoiding cancer

Lots of people think of cancer as a mystery. We all understand how you get malaria and the steps you can take to avoid it. We all understand how you get typhoid and what you can do to avoid it. And yet many of us think of cancer as something that, by and large, comes out of the blue. Either you're lucky or you're unlucky. Well, in fact, cancer is a lot less mysterious than you might imagine. The reality is that scientists now know a huge amount about how you 'catch' cancer. And how you can, in many cases, try to avoid it.

You can, as it were, catch cancer by contact with a carcinogen – a cancer-causing substance. It could be a man-made chemical or it could be something that occurs naturally. The bad news is that we're all exposed to carcinogens every day. The good news is that our bodies' defences normally overcome them. But if the level of exposure is too high, or too prolonged, especially at a time when the immune system is weak, then the body's defences may not be able to cope and cancer might develop. It's not just impractical, it's actually impossible to avoid all carcinogens. But it's just common sense to keep exposure to the minimum.

Many of us are exposed to carcinogens in our jobs. Research carried out in the European Union identified six common workplace carcinogens. Ranked by the number of people affected they are:

1 *solar radiation*
2 *tobacco smoke*
3 *crystalline silica*
4 *diesel exhaust*
5 *radon*
6 *wood dust.*

It's important to stress that a substance can be carcinogenic at certain concentrations but perfectly safe at lower concentrations. For example, all of us are exposed to solar radiation to some degree and, in the right quantity, it's beneficial to health. Nor is anybody going to get cancer by driving a diesel car or sawing some planks to make shelves at home.

The full list of proven or suspected carcinogens is extremely long. Here are some more of the common ones:

▶ *acrylamide (produced when carbohydrates are fried or overheated)*
▶ *aflatoxins (produced by a fungus that grows on grains and nuts)*
▶ *alcohol*
▶ *asbestos*
▶ *benzene*
▶ *cadmium*
▶ *charred food, especially charred meat residue on barbecues*
▶ *coal tar*
▶ *chlorophenols (a class of chemicals found in some herbicides and pesticides)*
▶ *diethanolamine (DEA) (found in some washing-up liquids, cosmetics and toiletries)*
▶ *radiation*
▶ *soot.*

Insight

There are so many known and possible carcinogens in so many products that it just isn't possible to detail them all here. The general rule is **read instructions carefully and follow all safety advice.**

What is cancer?

It's estimated that every strand of DNA is damaged every eight seconds or so. Fortunately, cells have mechanisms for repairing the damage. But when things go wrong, damaged cells can reproduce out of control to produce malignant tumours.

But why should a lump kill you? Or even make you ill? After all, we often develop lumps and bumps for all sorts of reasons and they're not harmful.

(Contd)

Indeed, you may have a malignant tumour for some time without being aware of it and without it causing any problems. It's not uncommon for a tumour to have been growing for 15 or 20 years before being discovered. But eventually the tumour becomes so large that it prevents the body functioning correctly. What's more, cancerous cells can break off and lodge in other parts of the body where they may cause additional tumours. Eventually, the body can no longer function at all.

Why does this happen? What is it that attacks the DNA? Well, it can be many things. It could be a carcinogenic chemical, for example, or a virus. To put the risk into perspective, it takes several gene mutations (unrepaired DNA damage) to produce cancer. Not just one. In fact, there's thought to be only one fatality for every 100 million billion cell divisions. Looked at like that, cancer is rare. But the more carcinogens we're exposed to, and the longer we live, the greater the risk.

Smoking – please stop

Jeanne Calment gave up smoking when she was 117 but took it up again at 118. When she died at the age of 122 she – as far as it can be proved – had lived longer than anyone else, *ever*. She was succeeded as the world's oldest person by Marie-Louise Meilleur, a smoker into her nineties. John McMorran was born in a log cabin in Michigan in 1889. He died in 2003 at the age of 113. He smoked cigars. And there have been plenty of other long-lived smokers, too.

Is that proof that smoking is harmless? Or, indeed, even beneficial?

Well, actually, no. You see, some people *are* pretty unaffected by smoking. But they're the exceptions. Something in their genes predisposes them to resistance to cancer and to longevity. Do you know for a fact that you have such genes? If you're not 100 per cent positive you'd better not take the risk. And you can't be, given the current state of knowledge about genes. Around 114,000 people in the UK die as a result of smoking every year. That's one-fifth of all UK deaths. It's a huge number. If you smoke, your best chance of prolonging your life is simply to give up.

Smoking is a gamble and here are the odds. Half of all smokers survive beyond 70. But – and it's a big but – the half of smokers who die *before* they're 70 lose, on average, *21 years of life*. So, if you smoke, you've got a 50:50 chance of losing 21 years. It's like tossing a coin. Heads, you're fine; tails, you lose two decades of your life. Or take roulette. You put your life on the red. If red comes up, you're fine. If black comes up, you lose about a quarter of the life you could have enjoyed. Or playing Russian roulette using a pistol with six chambers, three of them loaded. Would you really do any of those things?

Actually, it's worse than that. Because even if you survive beyond 70 you won't really be 'fine' at all. Yes, you'll be alive but you'll nevertheless suffer a whole range of unnecessary health problems. For every death caused by smoking, another 20 smokers suffer a smoking related disease. That doesn't make living longer a lot of fun.

It may surprise you to know that the number one problem you face if you smoke isn't cancer – it's heart disease. As early as 1958, American researchers Hammond and Horn made a statistical study of 187,783 men and discovered that the mortality of one-pack-a-day smokers from coronary heart disease was equivalent to that of non-smokers who were seven years older. Even those on a modest six cigarettes a day lost, on average, four years. If you're still smoking half a century after Hammond and Horn, don't you think it's time you caught up with their findings?

> Almost a third of all cancer deaths in the developed world are related to tobacco products.

The tar in cigarette smoke contains something called Benzo A-Pyrene-Diol-Epoxide (BPDE) that suppresses the p53 gene. That's a gene that protects against cancer. Once it's switched off, you can get cancer *anywhere* in your body, not just the lungs.

If you smoke, here are some of the risks you run:

- ▶ *heart disease*
- ▶ *various cancers including cancers of the lung, mouth, nose, larynx, throat, stomach, liver, pancreas, kidney, bladder and cervix*
- ▶ *respiratory complaints*
- ▶ *a 50 per cent higher risk of erectile dysfunction in men*
- ▶ *decreased bone density*
- ▶ *increased risk of fractures*
- ▶ *lumbar disc problems and low back pain*
- ▶ *decreased wound-healing ability*
- ▶ *premature ageing of the skin*
- ▶ *loose teeth*
- ▶ *a lowering of the calm-promoting hormone serotonin (in other words, smoking will not calm your nerves).*

HOW TO PROTECT YOURSELF

Some people give up smoking relatively easily. For others, it's incredibly difficult. That's not surprising because tobacco is one of the most powerfully addictive substances known. Nicotine significantly increases dopamine – the 'pleasure chemical' – in the brain. Stopping smoking therefore leads to a fall in dopamine and a tendency towards depression, until the body adjusts itself. No one wants to feel depressed, which is why quitting can be so hard. Do everything you can during this period to keep your dopamine up – in other words, treat yourself to life's many other pleasures. Pleasure is what it's all about.

Here are 15 tips for giving up:

1 *Treat yourself in other ways.*
2 *If you're in a smoking household, try to get everyone else to give up with you.*

3 *Prepare yourself mentally. You'll probably go through a period of craving, poor concentration, irritability and low spirits. But it won't last long.*

4 *Decide whether you're going to give up at once (generally the most effective) or cut down gradually.*

5 *If you suspect you may need some extra help (or know for sure from a previous attempt), try nicotine replacement therapy. Patches, lozenges, gum or inhalers roughly double your chance of success. You might also like to telephone a helpline or join a support group.*

6 *Make a date and stick to it – if you're a woman, your 'quit day' should be during the first half of your menstrual cycle.*

7 *On the day, some people find it helps to get rid of all ashtrays, lighters and cigarettes. Others feel more confident having a packet of cigarettes in their pockets. You'll have to decide what's best for you.*

8 *Keep busy with work and pleasure.*

9 *Drink plenty of fluids – always have a glass of, say, fruit juice handy.*

10 *Keep away from places where the temptation to smoke would be high; indulge in other pleasurable alternatives.*

11 *Be prepared to put on a little weight because quitting smoking slows the metabolism – but it's a small price to pay if it happens.*

12 *When you feel like putting something in your mouth, chew gum or a sweet or snack on fruit.*

13 *Exercise a little more than you've been used to – it'll help keep your weight from going up, increase your dopamine level and keep your mind off smoking. And make it fun.*

14 *Keep aside the money you're saving and use it to treat yourself from the very first day.*

15 *At the end of every day without smoking, reflect on your achievement and the immediate health and financial benefits.*

Insight

Is it worth quitting if you've been a long-term smoker? Most definitely. In just a year your risk of coronary heart disease will have fallen by half, according to the American Heart Association, and your lung function will be at least 10 per cent higher.

If you need more encouragement, don't forget that if you smoke you're not only damaging your own health but also that of anyone you live with. Don't imagine that the impact on non-smoking members of the family is trivial. Far from it. So-called second-hand smoke is potentially *more* dangerous than the smoke inhaled directly by the smoker because the smouldering tip of the cigarette burns at a lower temperature and the smoke doesn't pass through a filter. Of course, ultimately, the impact depends on the concentration of smoke in the air other people are breathing, but it's a serious health hazard.

If you don't smoke yourself but live with someone who does, ask them to smoke outside. Given the serious dangers of second-hand smoke, it isn't unreasonable.

Insight

A friend of mine refuses to give up smoking because, she says, she's not going to give in to persuasion. What she's overlooked is that the tobacco companies use even more powerful techniques of persuasion – and, unlike her relatives and friends, their motive is profit.

Viruses

Certain viruses are also carcinogens. They include:

▶ **Hepatitis B virus (hepadnavirus):** *This can cause liver cancer and is transmitted by sex or contact with contaminated blood. Effective treatments are available and most healthy people clear their infections.*
▶ **Hepatitis C virus (flavivirus):** *This can cause liver cancer and is also transmitted by sex or contact with contaminated blood. Treatment can reduce the virus to undetectable levels.*
▶ **Human papillomaviruses:** *More than 100 human papillomavirus types have been identified, of which several are associated with cervical cancer. Women with very healthy immune systems seem to be able to eliminate the virus within two years but in others the virus remains in the body indefinitely.*

HOW TO PROTECT YOURSELF

The best ways of protecting yourself against these viruses are:

- ▶ *Be monogamous. If you're not in a committed relationship, be cautious in your choice of sexual partners and use condoms.*
- ▶ *Don't share things like razor blades (which could have traces of contaminated blood on them).*
- ▶ *Make sure needles for injections or tattoos and similar items have been sterilized.*
- ▶ *Wear surgical gloves if treating a wound of someone you know to be infected with hepatitis.*
- ▶ *Have yourself vaccinated against hepatitis B if you know you're at risk. There is no vaccine for hepatitis C.*
- ▶ *Have regular cervical screening (human papillomavirus type 16 and type 18).*

Alcohol

A little alcohol may be good for you, as we saw in Chapter 2, but a lot of alcohol definitely isn't. In fact, alcohol is a factor in around 8,000 UK deaths a year. So where does the line lie? According to Carole L. Hart who led a team of researchers at the University of Glasgow, the threshold for men is 11 drinks a week. Above this, the negative health effects outweigh any positive effects. Unfortunately, the study followed only men (6,000 for 21 years), but based on existing knowledge, it seems the threshold for women would be lower. If you think that's unduly restrictive, consider the findings of a study of one million middle-aged women conducted by a team under Naomi E. Allen at the Cancer Epidemiology Unit at the University of Oxford. Their research concluded that drinking more than one to two units *a week* increased the risk of a wide range of cancers. And a study by the French National Cancer Institute concluded that it was *daily* consumption, even of small quantities, that was the most dangerous.

Too much alcohol increases the risk of:

- *liver damage, ranging from fatty liver through to cirrhosis*
- *cancer of the liver, rectum, breast, mouth, pharynx, larynx and oesophagus*
- *heart disease*
- *stroke*
- *gout*
- *kidney failure*
- *malnutrition due to impaired absorption*
- *dementia*
- *obesity due to alcohol's high calorific value*
- *insomnia, anxiety and depression*
- *disturbance to blood sugar levels.*

HOW TO PROTECT YOURSELF

Based on the Hart research, men should aim for no more than 11 alcoholic drinks a week. For women the equivalent figure would probably be about seven. Based on the study by Naomi E. Allen and colleagues at the Cancer Epidemiology Unit at the University of Oxford, a safer figure would be no more than two units *per week* (and, presumably, three for men). Specifically, the risk increased by 15 cancers per thousand women per unit of alcohol per day, with around three-quarters of those cancers being in the breast. Since the level of alcohol consumption was self-reported it seems quite possible that the women were drinking more than they admitted but, nevertheless, the link between increased breast cancer and increased alcohol consumption is clear. Against that, there may be some offsetting benefits in terms of reduced cardiovascular disease.

For many of us, cutting down on alcohol is hard to do. Here are some tips to help you:

- *Try to limit those situations where drinking is normal; find other enjoyable alternatives.*

- *If you're embarrassed about not drinking much, you might find it easier to tell people you've given up entirely – most people respect that.*
- *Offer to be the driver on nights out – people respect that as well.*
- *If you're a beer drinker, drink halves instead of pints.*
- *If you're a wine drinker, you may find it helps to buy top quality wines and savour a small quantity.*
- *Think of the calories you'll be cutting out – at least 85 for every half-pint of beer or small glass of wine.*
- *Don't binge drink but don't drink daily, either.*

Insight

The best advice is to look on alcohol as something for special occasions a couple of times a week – that romantic dinner, the big family lunch, the night out with friends. (On any one day men shouldn't drink more than three to four units and women no more than two to three units.)

What is 'one drink'?

A drink, that's to say a unit of alcohol, is equivalent to:

- *half a pint of average-strength beer*
- *a small glass of wine at 9 per cent*
- *a standard pub measure of spirits (25 ml)*
- *a standard pub measure of fortified wine (50 ml).*

Warning

If you're a heavy drinker, don't stop suddenly – the shock to your body could be dangerous. Instead, aim to cut down gradually.

Drugs

It should go without saying that the use of illegal drugs is incompatible with both living longer and living well. It's true that alcohol is the number one drug throughout most of the Western world and is responsible for more deaths than any other. But illegal drugs can be deadly, too. They're responsible for something like 1,600 deaths a year in the UK. If you're using illegal drugs, try to stop. If you can't stop on your own, seek help.

Sunshine

Sunshine is marvellous. It can lower blood pressure. It acts on sterols in the skin to produce vitamin D. It gives skin an attractive glow. It produces the tan that most of us crave. It increases the production of serotonin, the hormone that helps us feel cheerful and calm. And it generally makes us feel good.

But – there's almost always a but – sunshine can also kill, because the ultraviolet rays are carcinogenic. As with so many things, it's all a question of degree.

Skin cancer is the most common cancer in the UK. There are three main kinds:

1 **Melanoma.** *This is the most dangerous because it can spread to other parts of the body. It usually develops from a mole.*
2 **Squamous cell carcinoma.** *This affects the topmost layer of the skin and looks like a scaly patch.*
3 **Basal cell carcinoma.** *This affects the innermost layer of the skin and looks similar to squamous cell carcinoma.*

HOW TO PROTECT YOURSELF

Unless you're extremely fair it's not necessary to avoid sunshine altogether. The rules are:

- *Never allow your skin to burn.*
- *Try to build up a little bit of a protective tan before you go on that foreign beach holiday.*
- *On your first day on the beach avoid the midday sun and don't sunbathe for more than a few minutes at a time.*
- *Use an artificial tanner if you want to look brown on the first day – but don't forget that most fake tans give no protection.*
- *You can spend longer in the sun if you use a sunscreen, but don't take the protection factors too literally.*
- *If you're a bald man wear a hat.*
- *Children under three should always be protected from the sun – damage in infancy can lead to skin cancer later.*
- *Check your moles regularly and see your doctor if you notice any that are:*
  - ▷ *getting bigger*
  - ▷ *changing colour*
  - ▷ *developing ragged edges*
  - ▷ *becoming itchy*
  - ▷ *painful*
  - ▷ *bleeding.*

REPAIRING THE DAMAGE

Never proceed on the basis that skin damage can be undone. It's simply too risky. However, if you do have sun damage there's evidence that resveratrol (see page 75), both taken internally and applied directly in the form of a cream, can help.

Insight
Although you can spend longer in the sun if you use sunscreen, some scientists think its ingredients could actually cause skin cancer; pending further research the safest advice is to simply cut down on sunbathing.

Driving

Something like a quarter of a million people are injured on Britain's roads every year. Which means that in a lifetime you have, very roughly, a one in three chance of being among them. Just over 10 per cent of those accidents are classed as serious and around 3,000 people die each year. Nevertheless, the UK is one of the safest places on the planet to drive a car. The USA is significantly less so, with a per capita death rate almost three times higher (although its record isn't quite so bad in terms of deaths related to distance travelled).

HOW TO PROTECT YOURSELF

Here are a few tips to keep you safe:

- ▶ *Wear your seat belt – and make sure everyone else does.*
- ▶ *Adjust your head restraint correctly – it should be aligned with your head, not your neck.*
- ▶ *Don't leave loose objects inside your car – they could become dangerous projectiles.*
- ▶ *Choose a car with ABS (anti-skid) brakes and airbags.*
- ▶ *Leave in plenty of time and drive slowly.*
- ▶ *Drive predictably.*
- ▶ *Leave plenty of space between you and the vehicle in front.*
- ▶ *Know where your blind spots are – and recognize that other drivers have them too.*
- ▶ *Stay calm – if you find yourself getting stressed, stop.*
- ▶ *Don't get distracted.*
- ▶ *Slow down in rain, snow and fog.*
- ▶ *Be willing to yield to other drivers.*
- ▶ *Don't drive while under the influence of drink or drugs, including prescription drugs.*
- ▶ *Maintain your tyres and everything else about your vehicle.*
- ▶ *Use extreme care when overtaking – don't take chances.*
- ▶ *Be wary of overtaking slow or stopped vehicles – there may be a hazard ahead.*
- ▶ *Don't try to stop others passing you.*
- ▶ *Make rest stops on long journeys.*

Avoid head injury

It probably sounds rather odd to advise anyone to 'avoid head injury'. After all, people don't usually go about trying to get head injuries. Head injuries are *accidents*.

Well, yes, but there are always things you can do to reduce the risk of accidents. And there are other things you can do to protect yourself just in case an accident should happen.

Not many people are boxers – which is good – because boxers suffer a great deal of head injury. In 1990 a neuropathologist in Glasgow called Gareth Roberts studied boxers and found their brains were riddled with a substance called beta-amyloid, exactly the same dangerous substance found in the brains of those with Alzheimer's disease. Further research has confirmed that traumatic brain injury (TBI) increases the level of beta-amyloid in the spinal fluid. At first there may be no sign of damage, but in the following weeks, microscopic signs of Alzheimer's type changes begin to appear and, years later, dementia may be the result.

▶ *It isn't necessary for the skull to be damaged for TBI to occur.*
▶ *Very roughly, TBI doubles your chance of developing dementia.*

If you're confused for more than 15 minutes after a head injury, or if you have a headache that won't go away, or if you've actually been knocked unconscious, you must see a neurologist.

HOW TO PROTECT YOURSELF

The first rule for protecting your head is to **wear a helmet** in all appropriate situations: when riding a bicycle, a motorbike or a horse and when taking part in sports.

Various studies have shown that helmets can be extremely effective. They reduce brain injury to cyclists, for example, by about four-fifths. Buy a model designed specifically for the activity and pay for the best – your brain is, after all, your most important part. Most helmets will protect the skull but you also need plenty of padding to absorb any blow and spread the impact, so your brain doesn't smash itself against the *inside* of your skull. Fortunately, wearing a helmet isn't as onerous as it used to be – nowadays they're stylish as well as comfortable.

Here are some other steps you should take:

▶ *If you have the choice, avoid jobs with a high risk of head injury.*
▶ *Choose a car with air bags, make sure the head restraint is properly adjusted, wear your seat belt and observe all the other tips given in the earlier 'driving' section.*

Sex

We'll be looking at sex and its surprising relationship to longevity in detail in Chapter 10, but it's worth noting here that cases of sexually transmitted infections (STIs) are rising in the middle-aged and older. That's because high divorce rates are launching the once happily-married back into the uncertainties of the dating game.

If you've met someone new the only sensible course is to use condoms. The new person in your life will also be wondering about the chances of contracting an STI from you, so there's no need to be hesitant about discussing the subject before you get into bed. If you're on the pill or other similar form of contraception, or if you're too old to conceive, there's no need to say so. Insist on a condom and if the man refuses, don't have sex. Some older men may find intercourse difficult with a condom (because of the lack of stimulation) but that's something you'll both just have to cope with for a while.

For how long? Well, the HIV antibody test doesn't give a reliable result until three months after a sexual encounter. So the wise course is to both have the full set of tests immediately and continue to use condoms until your health professional says it's safe to stop.

Is it worth having medical check-ups?

If you're feeling perfectly well, is there any point in being screened for diseases on the merest chance that they *might* be developing? Some people say yes. Others say no. Here are the arguments.

- ▶ **Against:** *The accuracy of screening varies considerably from one condition to another and therefore people may be worried unnecessarily by false positives and even subjected to harmful further tests and treatments.*
- ▶ **For:** *Early detection results in early treatment, before the disease has done too much damage and before a cancer has spread.*

In fact, there's no conclusive answer either way because it all depends on what part of the body is being tested and what the screening method is. There are clear advantages to some techniques and equally clear disadvantages to others. So let's take a look at some specific tests.

BLOOD TESTS

The routine checks are:

- ▶ *liver function*
- ▶ *blood count (for anaemia and immune system function)*
- ▶ *thyroid stimulating hormone (for under-active thyroid)*
- ▶ *cholesterol – ideally you want total cholesterol under 5 mmol/l; LDL level under 3 mmol/l; HDL level over 1 mmol/l*
- ▶ *triglycerides – a high level is associated with the risk of coronary artery disease; ideally you want to be under 2 mmol/l*
- ▶ *glucose – an elevated level is indicative of diabetes mellitus*

▶ *prostate specific antigen (PSA) – an elevated level* may *be associated with prostate cancer.*

Conclusion
With the exception of the PSA test (dealt with separately below) these are uncontroversial. If the results are worse than you would have hoped, you'll be able to improve your prospects with simple lifestyle changes.

Insight
If your blood test requires that you can't have anything other than water for eight hours before the sample is taken, arrange an appointment for first thing in the morning.

PROSTATE CANCER

The test for prostate specific antigen (PSA) in the blood is controversial because a substantial proportion of men with raised levels do not have prostate cancer, while a small percentage will be negative despite having cancer. So there's the possibility of a good deal of unnecessary anguish.

Conclusion
Have the test if:

▶ *a close relative has had prostate cancer*
▶ *you have difficulty urinating/the flow is weak*
▶ *you have to get up several times a night.*

URINE TESTS

The two standard tests are:

1 **Sugar** – *for diabetes mellitus.*
2 **Protein** – *can indicate kidney or blood pressure problems or infection.*

Conclusion
Have the tests, if they are indicated.

VISION

Most people have got used to having their sight tested by middle age. The tests are harmless and if problems show up they can usually be managed. Make sure your eye pressure is tested. High pressure is associated with glaucoma, a potentially serious condition which can usually be treated with drops.

Conclusion
Have your eyes tested regularly.

HEARING

Sitting in a soundproof booth to exclude external noise, you'll be subject to sounds at various frequencies. As with vision tests, the process is harmless. If a hearing aid is proposed there are nowadays many excellent and unobtrusive models to choose from.

Conclusion
If you suspect you have a hearing problem then have the test.

BOWEL CANCER

The stool examination is one of the more controversial tests because only one out of ten positive results will actually be due to cancer. It would be better for your peace of mind to go straight to stage two, if possible, and have a colonoscopy to look at the interior of your bowel.

Conclusion
A colonoscopy is worthwhile for men and women over 50 and annually for those who have a close relative with bowel cancer. But if the stool examination is offered as the first step then that's the way you'll have to go.

PELVIC EXAMINATION AND CERVICAL SMEAR

The doctor will examine your vagina, ovaries and womb; and cells will be collected from the neck of the womb using a spatula.

If abnormal cells are found you'll need a follow-up test called a colposcopy. Removing the abnormal cells can usually be done simply and quickly by cryotherapy (freezing).

Conclusion
This is one of the tests with proven benefits in terms of longevity because abnormal cells can be detected long before cancer has developed and while treatment is easy and successful.

BREASTS

A mammogram can detect lumps in the breast which are too small to feel. The arguments against screening are that the majority of lumps are not cancerous and that, even when they are, treatment is often unnecessary (because of the slow rate of development compared with the woman's age). Some authorities have put the level of 'over-diagnosis' as high as 54 per cent but recent Swedish research put the figure at 10 per cent. What's more, the X-rays themselves pose such a health risk that screening shouldn't be repeated for two to three years.

Against all that, treatment is improving all the time and the earlier it begins the higher than likelihood of success.

Conclusion
Every woman should consider screening at recommended intervals.

BLOOD PRESSURE

Machines for measuring blood pressure are available so cheaply that it's worth buying your own. They'll tell you your systolic blood pressure (the highest) and the diastolic (the lowest) as well as your pulse. You'll probably find your pressure at home is lower than the reading the doctor gets. Optimum blood pressure is 120/80 or less but, as you get older, if you can keep yours under 130/85 your risk of either heart attack or stroke will be extremely small.

Conclusion

Everybody should know their blood pressure. If yours is too high it can be treated with tablets. Lifestyle choices that help reduce blood pressure have already been described. They include:

▶ *a diet high in fruits, vegetables, garlic, oily fish, calcium, oats, barley and olive oil*
▶ *a diet low in saturated fat and salt*
▶ *low weight*
▶ *a supplement of vitamin E*
▶ *low alcohol consumption*
▶ *regular exercise*
▶ *low stress.*

Body scans

Full or part body scans are now being offered by private health screening companies. They claim to offer peace of mind to the 'worried well' and the prospect of timely treatment for those who are found to have health problems. There are three different technologies:

1 *a computed tomography (CT) scan*
2 *a magnetic resonance imaging (MRI) scan*
3 *an ultrasound scan.*

CT scans are extremely good at detecting abnormalities. That's their strength but also their weakness. In one study of 1,200 whole-body CT scans, 87 per cent found at least one abnormality. Another study of 1,520 patients screened for lung cancer found that 700 abnormalities were detected that had nothing to do with lung cancer. On follow-up, the majority turned out to be false-positives. In fact, one estimate is that 80 per cent of abnormalities detected by CT scans are not life-threatening.

CT scans use X-rays. The typical dose of radiation is 10 mSv, which is equivalent to about 100 chest X-rays. This dose is associated with an increased risk of fatal cancer of about one in 2,000 (compared with a lifetime risk of about one in five). So the effect isn't negligible. Moreover, to be effective in terms of preventative diagnosis, you'll need to have scans at regular intervals of, say, every three years, which obviously increases the risk. It's been estimated that if men start three-yearly screening at age 40, 0.4 per cent will actually die from radiation. The figure for women is even higher at 0.6 per cent.

MRI scans use magnets and radio waves to produce two- and three-dimensional pictures of the inside of the body. Abnormalities show up as darker or lighter than the surrounding tissue. They're particularly suitable for the spine and joints, the heart, the brain and for the detection of tumours. The technique can't be used on anyone who has any kind of metal implant, nor is it advisable for pregnant women because the effects on a developing foetus, if any, haven't been researched. If a dye is used an allergic reaction is possible. Otherwise MRI scans are safe.

Ultrasound scans send high frequency sound waves through body tissues and process the echoes to create an on-screen image. The technology is widely used in pregnancy but can equally be targeted at any soft tissues. Ultrasound scans can detect a variety of conditions from osteoporosis (using a heel densitometer), to aneurysms (a ballooning of a weak point of an artery) to the build-up of plaque in arteries, which might lead to strokes. No X-rays are employed and there are no known risks.

Conclusion
CT scans can cause a great deal of unnecessary distress and, because of the high dose of X-rays, actually increase health risks. They're not worthwhile for people who have no reason to suspect a problem.

MRI scans have little risk and ultrasound scans have no known risk. Nevertheless, there's no evidence that these scans are beneficial to apparently healthy people.

Of course, all these methods of scanning can be life savers when family histories or symptoms suggest there could be a problem. That's a different matter.

10 THINGS TO REMEMBER

1 *Prudence is an important quality if you want to live a long time.*

2 *Many of the causes of cancer can be avoided.*

3 *Half of all smokers lose an average of 21 years of their lives.*

4 *Some viruses cause cancer.*

5 *Alcohol and illegal drugs are a factor in thousands of deaths each year.*

6 *Skin cancer can be a killer, but is easily avoided.*

7 *You have roughly a one in three chance of being injured in a road accident in your lifetime, so drive carefully.*

8 *Always wear a helmet when taking part in dangerous activities.*

9 *Sexually transmitted infections are on the increase among the middle-aged and older: always use condoms with a new partner.*

10 *Some medical check-ups can save lives, but be selective – others can actually do more harm than good.*

HOW MUCH LONGER ARE YOU GOING TO LIVE NOW?

▶ *Are you aware of the most common carcinogens and are you avoiding them?*
▶ *Are you a non-smoker?*
▶ *Have you been vaccinated against hepatitis B and are you taking steps to protect yourself against hepatitis viruses?*
▶ *Are you drinking alcohol only in moderation and certainly not daily?*
▶ *Are you someone who doesn't take drugs?*
▶ *Are you getting enough sunshine to generate vitamin D, but without ever getting burnt?*
▶ *Are you a careful driver?*
▶ *Do you wear a helmet when taking part in dangerous sports?*
▶ *Do you practise safe sex?*
▶ *Do you have regular health checks as appropriate?*

Score:

If you answered 'yes' to seven or more questions you're obviously taking good care to avoid accidents and health risks, and that's very important for longevity. Move on to the next chapter.

If you answered 'yes' to between four and six questions you're well on the way to developing the right outlook and lifestyle but there's quite a bit more you could do. You can also move on to the next chapter but re-read this one from time to time with the aim of eventually putting everything into practice.

If you answered 'yes' to three or fewer questions then you're really leaving too much to chance. Carefully review the way you live with reference to this chapter and get you score up to at least four 'yesses' before moving on.

9

Love

In this chapter you will learn:
- *how relationships can lengthen your life*
- *how pets can improve your well-being*
- *how love can survive death.*

There's no proof that André Debry and his wife Marguerite lived longer together than they would have done separately. But you could safely bet on it. In August 2004 they celebrated their wedding anniversary. Not their fiftieth. Not their sixtieth. Nor even their seventieth. On 12 August 2004 they had been married 80 years.

And, in fact, they went on to celebrate 81 years. When Monsieur Debry, one of eight surviving First World War French soldiers known as *les poilus* (the hairy ones), died two weeks later their combined ages were 207.

Was it exercise? Was it food? Was it spirituality? It may have been all those things. But the Debrys also had something very special. Something that the more of it you give, the more you have and the more you get. What is this remarkable substance? It's called *love* and you probably won't get very old without it:

- ▸ *If you don't love yourself you won't look after yourself.*
- ▸ *If you don't love anyone or anything else your life won't have any point.*
- ▸ *If you take care of the first two, the third – being loved – comes automatically.*

Of course, that's not to say the Debrys loved more passionately than any other couple, but it is to say that if they hadn't loved they probably wouldn't have reached the ages they did.

That special someone

All relationships are good for us. Our degree of connection with other people is a key indicator of longevity. But it seems one type of relationship is more powerful than any other. That's the committed relationship between lovers.

A study by the University of New Mexico School of Medicine of 256 elderly people found that those who had a close one-to-one relationship were the healthiest. Somehow, being involved in a single, intimate relationship gave them stronger immune systems, better cardiovascular health and more endorphins (which suppress pain and, in sufficient quantity, create euphoria).

In fact, according to a study by Linda Waite, a sociologist at the University of Chicago, being married is about the easiest way of prolonging life. Especially for men.

For a man, living alone is particularly unhealthy. A man alone is three times more likely to suffer a mental disorder than a married man, while a divorced man is five times more at risk. Men without partners also suffer a far higher rate of various illnesses. A divorced or separated man, for example, is ten times more likely to die from TB than if he'd remained married and the death rates are also very significantly higher for cirrhosis, pneumonia and cancer of the mouth and throat. It all adds up to ten extra years for men who are married.

For women the figure is a less dramatic but still very significant four years. Women *whose partners are supportive* suffer far less from stress and depression than women who live alone. Another study discovered that women who were lonely had poor immune function.

Scientists at the University of California studied US census data and concluded that married couples are more likely to live to a very old age than the unmarried, divorced or widowed. In fact, people who never marry are almost two-thirds more likely to die prematurely, and the picture for single men is the worst of all.

Insight

In a sense, loneliness is a disease. We're social creatures and we need the company of others. In particular, we need people we can feel close to. People who care about us. People who support us when we have problems. People we can touch and be touched by.

Love is the food of health

It's a need that begins the day we're born. In the 1940s, René Spitz made a pioneering study of infants in orphanages and compared them with those born in and living in prison with their mothers. Within two years of beginning his research, even though the standards of hygiene, medical care and nutrition were good, 37 per cent of the infants in the orphanages were dead. None of the infants in prison were. Spitz concluded that the infants essentially died from a lack of love.

In another study, Harold Skeels demonstrated the benefits of removing infants from orphanages and placing them with surrogate mothers who would love them. Three decades later he set out to discover what had become of them all. Although the infants had been classified as 'mentally retarded' (the term of the time), he found they were all living normally in the community and had an average IQ of 92. Meanwhile, the infants who had been left behind in the orphanages were either dead or still institutionalized.

The need to be loved, and to love, never leaves us. A study by Sam Sisca, Patricia Walsh and Anthony Walsh asked people to rate to what extent they felt loved or unloved. They discovered that the more someone felt unloved the higher their blood pressure. And, significantly, the effect was increasingly marked with age, suggesting to the researchers that years of love deprivation had had a cumulative effect.

Most of us have that feeling we're not complete when we're alone. It's reflected in many creation stories. In Hinduism, for example, in the beginning there was the ONE. But the ONE was lonely and therefore created a companion. In the Bible, God created man and then decided it was not good for man to be alone. So he created woman. And the Bible says the two must become one flesh. That's how the vast majority of us feel. We want to be *united*. Alone, life seems to have little point.

More love, less stress

How can a lack of love and human warmth explain physical symptoms? How can love deprivation raise blood pressure? How can it depress immune function? How can love itself make people healthier? It may sound like a lot of New Age hocus-pocus but, in fact, science has uncovered the very simple pathways that make the holistic approach an inescapable reality.

A lot of it is to do with stress. People who feel unloved have a low resistance to stress. People who feel loved have a high resistance. A fascinating illustration of this was provided in 2006 by a team led by Dr Anna Phillips at the University of Birmingham. Happily married volunteers were stressed by being given a mental arithmetic test in their homes. When their partners were in the room, blood pressure and heart rates were lower. When the subjects were alone, however, blood pressure and heart rate went up and, what's more, performance went down. Interestingly, the effect was more marked for women than men.

Stress, as we saw in Chapter 6, causes the secretion of adrenaline (epinephrine) and noradrenaline (norepinephrine), and raises the level of fatty lipids in the blood. If the stress goes on for years the result is arteriosclerosis – hardening and narrowing of the arteries – leading to chronically high blood pressure. Stress also pushes up cortisol (a stress-related hormone that depresses the immune system) and has damaging effects on the cardiovascular, gastrointestinal, respiratory and endocrine (hormonal) systems.

We all know of the phrase 'died of a broken heart'. And, in fact, it can literally be true: lovelessness can lead to illness, including heart problems.

Insight

On the Holmes-Rahe Life Change Scale the most stressful events are all to do with *personal relationships*. The most stressful thing that can happen to anybody is the death of a spouse, which is rated as 100. That's followed by divorce, separation and the death of a close family member. So stress is, above all, a 'disease' of loneliness and lovelessness.

Psychoneurosexuality

Dr Paul Pearsall had cancer of the lymph nodes that spread to his bones. He had chemotherapy, he had radiation, he had surgery. As he came round from an operation he actually heard a doctor say: 'I think we've lost him.'

It was then, according to his own account, that he became aware of his wife's breath on his cheek. He felt her tears falling on his eyelids. He felt her fingers touching his arms, chest, and the scars on his abdomen. And he heard her say: 'I love you. I'm here.'

At that moment he experienced a kind of revelation. He understood that the whole point of life is to *connect*. As intensely, intimately and sensuously as possible. When you're very ill, he realized, the most important thing is to be seen, heard, touched and understood by another loving person.

At the time of writing this, 20 years after that moment of revelation, Dr Pearsall is still alive.

Dr Pearsall was a clinical psychoneuroimmunologist – a specialist in the brain's interaction with the immune system. He now invented what he called psychoneurosexuality, the study of the relationship between the brain, the mind, the immune system and the sexual system.

We'll be looking at sex in the next chapter. As regards your immune system, it comprises about a trillion lymphocytes and 100 million trillion antibodies. And here's a curious thing. Your skin is actually the largest part of it. Effectively, when you touch somebody, you touch them with your immune system. Dr Pearsall believes that when people live together, their immune systems are actually connected to and interacting with one another's (just as when women live together their cycles tend to become synchronized).

In his view, the brain probably shouldn't be thought of as existing only inside the skull, and the mind certainly shouldn't be thought of as existing only inside the brain. He believes the mind is more or less everywhere within the body.

In a way, we've always known it and yet never openly acknowledged it. The proof is our everyday use of phrases such as 'gut feeling', 'a pain in the neck', and 'breaking my heart'.

And that's a view bolstered by a team led by Gerard Karsenty of Columbia University. In 2007 they discovered that the skeleton acts as a part of the endocrine system, which uses hormones to send signals. That's another way of saying that even the skeleton is effectively part of the mind. Incredible!

One of the most fascinating hormones of the 'body-as-mind' is oxytocin.

Oxytocin

There's good evidence that, apart from anything else, oxytocin can help you live longer. It's certainly been proven to extend the life of rats. And, so far, no one has found anything wrong with it, other than its curious tendency to make people forgetful. On the contrary, it has some marvellous effects, such as increasing your sense of attachment to your partner. In fact, it might be called the marital satisfaction molecule. (And it can similarly improve your relationships with your children – and anyone else you're close to.)

So where can you get hold of this wonderful substance? The good news is you don't even have to go to the shops. It's free. It's actually secreted by your own pituitary gland. To improve your chances of reaching 100 or more, all you need to do is increase the output. Unfortunately, you have no direct control over your pituitary. However, there is a special indirect technique you can learn.

Here it is. Are you ready? Take your hand and place it on the skin of the person you love. Yup, that's all there is to it. Of course, now you know that, you can always work out your own ways of improving the basic technique. But the essence of it is simply *touching*. When you touch someone you love, or someone you love touches you, your oxytocin level rises.

Oxytocin's extraordinary role began when you were born. It was responsible for your mother's contractions; it was responsible for making milk flow from her breasts; it was responsible for making her maternal and your father paternal; it made your parents more likely to stick together and it was why they didn't chuck you out when you cried for the hundredth time in a day. On top of all that, it helped your brain develop properly – without it some of your brain cells would have died. So if it hadn't been for *touch* and oxytocin your life would have been very different.

Try this

Get touching and hugging at once. Here's what to do *right now*:

▶ *If you have a partner, give him or her a hug. Find some place you can put your hand on bare skin.*

▶ *If you have children give them a hug. If they refuse to be hugged then, at least, deliver a slap on the back or a squeeze of the shoulders; the very minimum is a high five.*

▶ *If you have parents, sisters, brothers, whatever, give them all a hug.*

▶ *If you have a dog or a cat or any cuddly pet, go and stroke it.*

▶ *If there's a tree or some long grass, feel it with your hand.*

Insight

If you have a pet, count the number of times you stroke it in a day. Then count the number of times you touch your partner. If your dog or cat is getting more physical affection than your partner (or your children) there's something wrong. You need to make sure the humans you're close to get at least as much touching as your pet. You see, we often forget that we, too, are animals and need to touch and be touched. Why should we have less of this wonderful tonic than a dog does? We cover our bodies completely with clothes most of the time, which already makes it difficult and, on top of that, we've introduced dangerous social conventions. That we've now become afraid to touch one another is a disaster for oxytocin, happiness and longevity.

Improving your relationship

Of course, having a partner doesn't automatically contribute to longevity. It's the *nature* of the relationship that counts. Indeed, a bad relationship might even contribute to various diseases and shorten both your lives. Love is a skill that, like any skill, has to be learned and then practised conscientiously. Here are 15 guidelines for a relationship that will enhance happiness, health and longevity for both of you:

1 **Accept your partner's love.** *Don't insist it has to be expressed in a particular way. You have to be free to express your love your way and your partner has to be free to do the same. Simply* enjoy *the love.* Bathe *in it.* Be grateful *for it, because it's a wonderful thing.*

2 **Accept the way your partner is.** *Don't tell your partner how to dress or behave or what to think or, indeed, anything else. In other words, don't project your fantasies onto your partner.*

3 **Accept your partner's growth.** *Don't try to keep your partner the way they were right back at the beginning of the relationship. You both have to be free to develop. In fact, learn to love change. Because if there was no change there could be no improvement. Would you, at, say, age 40, really want your partner to be the same as when you first met 20 years earlier? Not to know any more? Not to have acquired any more skills? Not to have more insight and wisdom?*

4 **Accept that two people are different and always will be** *(especially if one is a man and the other a woman). You already love some of the differences. Learn to love* all *of them.*

5 **Always remain curious about your partner.** *He or she is actually an inexhaustible mine. You'll never run out of treasures as long as you keep digging new galleries.*

6 **Always give support.** *This is very important for both sexes but especially for women who have a strong need to be able to talk about themselves and their problems. In one study, 41 per cent of women who suffered a 'stressful life event' became depressed if they were given only a low level of support by their partners but the figure fell to 10 per cent if they had a high level of support. Another study found that relationships in which partners react enthusiastically to one-another's good news are the happiest – don't be grudging or uninterested.*

7 **Always build your partner up.** *Negative thoughts and emotions can be damaging and if you foster them in your*

partner – possibly as a way of gaining dominance in the relationship – you'll end up destroying him or her. Don't criticize and, above all, never make personal attacks.

8 **Talk, talk, talk.** *And when you talk, give all of your attention. Communicate, don't sulk. As soon as there's a problem, be willing to discuss it. One study found that talking to a woman is more meaningful than talking to a man. Both men and women reported that talking to a woman resulted in a conversation that was more pleasant, more intimate and – this is very important – had more self-disclosure. So, if you're a man, learn to be meaningful.*

9 **Don't make comparisons.** *Don't say or even think 'He earns more money than my partner.' Or 'She's more beautiful than my partner.'*

10 **Don't hold onto negative thoughts or emotions.**

11 **Provide plenty of physical contact.** *As we saw above, oxytocin is essential to your health as well as the health of your relationship.*

12 **Have plenty of sex.** *Sex is the source of several 'happy chemicals'. One study found that satisfaction with a relationship correlates very closely with frequency of intercourse minus the number of rows.*

13 **Do something special together every day.**

14 **Take care of your partner.** *It's well known that, on average, women live longer than men. Various theories as to why this should be so have been put forward, but it's possible that something as simple as caring could be part of the explanation. The female is the caring sex and it is caring love that's the most important.*

15 **Merge with your partner.** *Think in terms of 'us' and not in terms of 'you' and 'me'. Think of your personal health as the product of your joint health. Every day 'send' your mind inside your partner; try to sense what your partner's thinking and feeling. Develop a spiritual connection with your partner and with all of the universe (see Chapter 11).*

Try this

Draw a line down the middle of some sheets of paper from top to bottom. On the left, make a list of all the differences you have with your partner. On the right, set out all the things that are puzzling about those differences, but also all the things that are wonderful about them. Have your partner do the same. Then discuss what you've written.

If your partner has died

Quite apart from anything else, the death of a partner is something that's very bad for your own health. A study led by R. W. Bartop found the immune systems of men and women whose partners had recently died were functioning far below the normal level. And a 1978 train crash in Australia which killed 26 men led psychiatrist Roger Barthrop to the discovery that their widows' lymphocytes (part of the immune system) became less numerous and less active.

If your partner has died that doesn't mean, of course, that love itself has died. You can still love your partner, even if he or she is no longer physically present. Continue to think about your partner. Talk to your partner. Keep your reminders. Don't let younger people convince you it isn't healthy to behave that way. Quite frankly, it's something younger people just can't understand. So there's really no point in listening to them. It *isn't* unhealthy.

What's unhealthy is to feel alone. With your memories you're not alone. After the artist-poet and mystic William Blake died in 1827 his wife said he visited her for two or three hours every day, sitting in 'his chair'. She herself died four years later, calling out to him to say she was coming.

Eventually you may feel it right to feel new love with a new partner. If that's the case, there's no need to feel guilt. We need to love and be loved all our lives.

Relatives and friends

A close one-to-one relationship may be the most powerful of all but, of course, all relationships are beneficial. William Knaus and his team at the George Washington University School of Medicine analysed the treatment of more than 5,000 patients in intensive care in various hospitals throughout the USA and found the single most important factor in recovery was the degree of human contact between nurses and patients. Where there was hand-holding and reassurance the outcomes were good. Where there was no time for such 'luxuries' the outcome was poor. Millions of dollars' worth of modern technology counted for less than old fashioned, free human warmth.

In a study by Dr David Spiegel of women whose breast cancers had spread, those who regularly attended a support group did better than those who didn't.

Try this
If you're not intimate with someone then, by definition, you're separated from that person. If you're not intimate with anybody then you're lonely.

- ▶ *Don't wait for someone else to be friendly – be the first.*
- ▶ *Don't wait for someone else to introduce an intimate subject – be the first.*
- ▶ *Don't wait for someone else to make a personal disclosure – be the first.*
- ▶ *The more you give the more you get.*

If you want to get on well with other people, you have to push your happiness and your love ahead of you so they can easily see it.

You won't be able to push that aura ahead of you if you're a judgemental sort of person. Don't approach others with feelings of hostility or suspicion, with your positive emotions hidden away behind your back like some precious metal. Other people will sense it.

Remember, you can't empathize fully if you're harsh on people who are different from you. For example, if you've never smoked, you'll never understand someone who's addicted to nicotine unless you seek to understand it non-judgementally. Nor, unless you're open-minded, will you be able to relate to people from different social backgrounds, different cultures or different age groups. Obviously, you'll widen your circle of friends if you can understand those differences.

- ▶ *Be interested in other people.*
- ▶ *Be compassionate towards other people.*
- ▶ *Be responsive – use facial expressions and tone of voice.*
- ▶ *Trust people with small things and work up to big things – don't distrust people without reason.*
- ▶ *Don't be judgemental.*
- ▶ *Try to find something you agree with.*
- ▶ *If you disagree, mention the thing you agree with before mentioning the thing you disagree with.*

Insight

Of course, you could just confine your friendships to people with exactly the same background and outlook as yourself, but you'll be limiting your opportunities for happiness if you do. And there's one kind of difference most of us are anxious to bridge – that between the sexes.

Pets

I can put my hand out to my side day or night and he is always there. He has taught me to love, laugh and live again.

Those are moving words, describing exactly the kind of relationship we all want. But they are not the words of someone talking about their human partner, they are the words of Allen Parton, talking about Endal, his yellow Labrador retriever. And Mr Parton has a lot more to say:

His unconditional love has healed so many of the hurts; his mischief making brought laughter into my saddest days and his zest for life has rubbed off on to me. He never judges me...

It was a road accident in 1991 that put Mr Parton into a wheelchair. He had a wife and he had children and yet, even so, he was 'stuck in the darkest soulless place a person can ever be.' It took a dog, six years later, to pull him out.

And it's not only emotional support that Endal provided up until his death in 2009. Trained by Canine Partners for Independence, the dog could do all kinds of practical things that can extend the capabilities of elderly as well as disabled people. Endal could respond to one hundred instructions, including operating buttons and switches, loading and unloading a washing machine and pulling the plug out of the bath. As if that's not already incredible enough, Endal's actions in 2001 made him famous. After Mr Parton was struck by a car and thrown from his wheelchair, Endal got him into the recovery position, covered him with a blanket, brought a mobile phone and then went to a nearby hotel for help. The message is clear: if you don't have anyone to love, or love you, get a pet.

And, of course, even if you do have a loving partner, family and friends there's still room for a pet in your world.

Endal has certainly improved Allen Parton's life, and quite probably extended it, but is there any evidence that pets generally – pets that don't have that special training – can work that magic for everybody? In fact, there's plenty. Numerous studies have shown that pets can:

- ▶ *lower blood pressure*
- ▶ *lower cholesterol*
- ▶ *improve psychological health*
- ▶ *reduce visits to the doctor*
- ▶ *reduce stress*
- ▶ *aid recovery.*

In a famous study of heart attack victims, for example, a team at the University of Pennsylvania led by Erika Friedmann, showed that pet-owners were twice as likely to survive for a year compared with non-pet owners. The effects are so clear that many hospitals and hospices have animals that visit the patients. Surveys in Australia, Britain, Germany and the USA have all found health benefits from pet ownership.

What's the mechanism? Probably the most important thing is oxytocin. Just as with a human partner, when you stroke an animal the level goes up, increasing in turn the 'happy chemicals' dopamine and serotonin. But setting the biochemistry aside, you can just say it's love.

And the most important aspect of pet-love is that it doesn't depend on Fido being the most beautiful dog, nor the most intelligent, nor the most useful, nor anything like that. And Fido's love for you doesn't depend on your looks either, nor your wealth, nor the size of your house, nor anything of that kind. Basically, you love Fido because he loves you. And he loves you because you love him. It's love without other conditions. And that's what we all need.

Stories of the devotion of animals are legion. A terrier that remained for weeks by the body of its dead master in the Lake District in 1805 was commemorated in a painting by Landseer and in a poem by Wordsworth who recorded:

> *Yes, proof was plain that, since the day*
> *When this ill-fated Traveller died,*
> *The Dog had watched about the spot,*
> *Or by his master's side...*

Pets have two more important qualities. Firstly, they have the ability to 'see' emotions, which is why a dog disappears the morning before an appointment at the vet or why a horse refuses to be caught when it needs to be given an injection. When you interact with animals you have to learn to get rid of your negative emotions – *genuinely* get rid of them – because animals can read you like a book. That's how they survive. And when you've done that, your relationships with people will improve.

The second is that a pet, particularly a dog or a horse, is also a doorway back into the Nature from which so many of us are now unhappily estranged (although we'll probably never learn things like direction finding and earthquake prediction). I'll have more to say about this in Chapter 11.

Insight

You can't expect to get a pet today and feel instant benefits. You and your pet need to *bond* and that takes both time and an underlying feeling for a particular type of animal. Don't forget, either, that pets can sometimes *increase stress* if they're not properly trained to behave, if they turn out to be a burden, or if they, themselves, get ill. So you need to think very carefully about what pet will suit you.

Try this

Even if you have friends enough, and children, and relatives and a partner, you should still consider having a pet. If you're lonely, a pet is essential. What kind of pet is a matter for you to decide. But a pet that lives in the house is going to be a more constant source of all those benefits than one that lives outside. If you don't have any firm ideas, get a dog. Dogs became man's best friend at least 100,000 years ago, are always ready for a good cuddle and form really meaningful relationships with their owners. They come in all shapes and sizes and one of them will be right for you. And there's the bonus that taking Fido for a walk every day will improve your fitness.

Insight

If there's no way you can have a pet, try riding. Horses can be very frightening and intimidating at first but once you get used to them you can enjoy something you can't get from a dog or a cat. You can enjoy being *carried* which, for some people, is a very special experience.

Remember: a pet is for life

Don't forget that animals have to be properly looked after throughout their lives. If you're not 100 per cent sure you are able to do that then don't get a pet.

On the other hand, don't rule out a pet on the grounds that you're elderly and may die first. If that's your case, consider adopting an older cat or dog from a rescue centre. Then make firm arrangements for it to be taken care of should it outlive you.

How well connected are you?

As we've seen, it's important for your health and happiness and longevity to be connected to other people and animals. Here's a little test so you can see how well you're doing.

1 *Are you living with a partner in a close and happy relationship?*
2 *If not, do you live with someone else (parents, children, siblings, etc.)?*
3 *Have you got a pet with which you feel a special bond?*
4 *Have you got family members living within half an hour?*
5 *If not, do you regularly keep in touch by phone, email or post?*
6 *Do you visit family members at least once a week?*
7 *Do you have friends you see regularly?*
8 *Do you have a special friend with whom you can share your problems?*
9 *Do you socialize with colleagues from work?*
10 *Do you have a good laugh with family and friends?*
11 *Do you have a hobby that involves meeting people?*
12 *Do you do any voluntary or charitable work that involves helping other people?*

How did you get on?
Mostly yes: You're extremely sociable and well connected with all the benefits that brings.

Half yes, half no: You're moderately sociable but you'd gain a lot if you widened your circle.

Mostly no: whether by choice or circumstance you're cut off and need to make a real effort to socialize more widely.

10 THINGS TO REMEMBER

1 *Loving and being loved is vital for longevity.*

2 *The committed relationship between two partners is the most powerful of all.*

3 *Living alone is even more unhealthy for a man than a woman.*

4 *In any relationship, it's vital to be supportive.*

5 *If you feel unloved you suffer more stress.*

6 *Oxytocin, a hormone that's released when you touch someone you love, increases your sense of attachment and seems to play a role in living longer – so touch often.*

7 *Acceptance is the key to successful relationships.*

8 *Love can continue even after someone has died.*

9 *Don't wait for someone else to be friendly – be the first.*

10 *Pets can provide unconditional love and companionship.*

HOW MUCH LONGER ARE YOU GOING TO LIVE NOW?

▶ *Do you love yourself?*
▶ *Are there other people in your life for whom you feel love?*
▶ *Do you have a partner you love, and who loves you?*
▶ *Do you have plenty of skin-on-skin contact with your partner?*
▶ *Are there people in your life that you cuddle?*
▶ *Do you accept your partner as he or she is, and does your partner accept you the same way?*
▶ *Are you still finding out things about your partner, and is your partner still finding new things in you?*
▶ *Are you supportive of your partner and is your partner supportive of you?*
▶ *Do you have a pet you stroke and cuddle?*
▶ *Do you socialize with lots of different people?*

Score:

If you answered 'yes' to seven or more questions you're obviously lucky in every sort of love, and that's very important for longevity. Move on to the next chapter.

If you answered 'yes' to between four and six questions you're on the right lines, but there's quite a bit more you could do to find and give love. You can also move on to the next chapter but re-read this one from time to time with the aim of eventually putting everything into practice.

If you answered 'yes' to three or fewer questions, then you're at a time in your life when either you're very happy to be independent or you're very unhappy to be isolated (whether in or out of a relationship). If it's the former, move on – you will find love in time. If it's the latter, read through the chapter again and try to put as many recommendations as possible into effect. Aim to score four 'yesses' before moving on to the next chapter.

10

Sex

In this chapter you will learn:
- *how regular sex can lengthen your life by up to ten years*
- *how sex when you're older is actually better than sex when you're younger*
- *techniques for continuing an enjoyable sex life into old age.*

Francisco Repilado was contemplating the prospect of his birthday – one of the 'big os' – when he heard the American guitarist Ry Cooder was seeking him out. Cooder wanted to make an album of the style of music known as *son de Cuba* and Francisco, who sang, danced and played the guitar, was top of Cooder's list. Francisco wasn't then coming up for four o, nor five o, nor even six o. He was close to nine o. Ninety!

But, then, that's not so extraordinary on Cuba where, out of a population of 11 million, more than 3,000 are centenarians. In fact, the reputation of the island for longevity prompted Professor Nancy Nepomucemo to study the Cuban secret.

There's a clue in the lyrics of the song with which Francisco opened Cooder's album. 'The love I have for you,' he sang, 'I cannot deny. My mouth is watering. I just can't help myself.'

Yes, love and sex were Francisco's elixir of youth, along, he said, with cigars, rum and dancing. And Professor Nepomucemo confirmed it. Cubans of whatever age, she discovered, were unusually preoccupied with their sex lives.

The song was called 'Chan Chan', the album was *The Buena Vista Social Club*, and following its release in 1997 it sold more than five million copies. Francisco, in his trademark panama hat, became known around the world under his stage name of Compay Segundo, and relished the press reports of his astonishing virility.

It sounds incredible. And for many of us, too good to be true. Sex can do a lot but can it really help you live longer? The truth is, yes, it can.

In 1988, Dr David Weeks placed an advert in the *New Scientist* magazine asking people who looked and felt younger than their age to contact him. He interviewed more than 3,500 people, from ages 18 to 102, in Britain, Europe and the US. He concluded that genes were 25 per cent responsible for a youthful appearance (Compay's grandmother lived to 115) and, next in importance, were exercise and sex. Interestingly, 40 per cent of the men and 20 per cent of the women believed it was their active sex lives that helped keep them young. Dr Weeks concluded that a high quality sex life equated with four to seven years off the appearance.

But there are clear physical benefits to sex, too. In the previous chapter we saw the advantages of touch and oxytocin. Going further, a study by Dr Dudley Chapman at Ohio University College of Osteopathic Medicine found that women who were content with their sex lives had higher T cell levels – and therefore stronger immune systems – than those who weren't.

A study of 100 women who had suffered a heart attack found that two-thirds reported sexual dissatisfaction. And a study of 131 men found almost exactly the same proportion reporting sexual problems prior to their heart attacks. Another study, in and around Caerphilly in Wales, focusing on 918 men aged 45 to 59, found that those who had sex only infrequently suffered twice the mortality of those who had two or more orgasms a week. In the case of coronary heart disease the difference was especially marked. The study concluded that sex has the potential to extend life by *as much as a decade*.

Now, you may be thinking it was the healthiest people who had the most sex. In which case, they would be bound to live longer.

Or those with the strongest relationships. In which case, as we saw in the last chapter, they would also be favoured. Undoubtedly those are factors. But, even so, there are good scientific reasons why frequent, regular sex should directly promote youthfulness and longevity.

In fact, when you stop to think about it, it isn't very surprising at all. We now know all about the mind/body connection. When you yearn for physical intimacy with the person you love but don't have it, you feel miserable, irritable and rejected. In a word, you feel stressed. And stress, as everyone knows, leads to health problems. By contrast, when you enjoy regular physical intimacy, you feel more serene and happy.

In some cultures, and especially in Chinese Taoist thought, sexual energy *is* energy. If you generate sexual energy, you'll feel more vital in every way. And vitality is associated with longevity. That energy and sex are connected has been proven by numerous Western studies. Three-quarters of men who were put on an exercise programme for nine months reported they were having more sex by the end of it. In another study, middle-aged swimmers had more sex than non-exercisers. And in a survey of 8,000 American women by sex therapist Linda de Villiers, a quarter said sexual desire increased after exercise, a quarter said they climaxed faster after exercise, and a third said they had sex more often after exercise. Moreover, people subjectively feel a connection between sex and exercise; in other studies, two-thirds of cyclists and 80 per cent of runners believed exercise improved their sex lives.

Of course, none of that *proves* that having sex increases your energy levels generally. But the Taoists believed it – providing sex was done in the right way. We'll be taking a look at that in a moment.

If it's true that an active sex life promotes longevity, what would be the mechanism? It seems it could work in several ways:

▶ *Sex boosts testosterone levels in both men and women, which in turn increases energy.*

- *Sex boosts oestrogen in women, which improves skin tone, combats osteoporosis and heart disease, and acts as a mild antidepressant.*
- *Sex boosts human growth hormone, which can result in improved circulation, bone strength and immune-system function as well as reduced fat.*
- *Sex boosts dopamine and PEA which, apart from causing pleasure, may keep the brain young.*
- *Sex boosts vasopressin, which is associated with mental acuity and longevity.*
- *Sex boosts oxytocin, which elevates mood and may enhance longevity.*
- *Sex boosts the hormone DHEA, which is associated with lower levels of Alzheimer's.*
- *Sex provides some exercise.*

Of course, it's not just any old sex that will bring the maximum benefit. It has to be good sex in the context of a loving relationship – and that's especially important for women.

Insight

Chen Dong of Chongqing in China stopped having sex with his wife Yu Hui for 17 years and eventually the couple divorced. He also gave up meat. The reason? He believed that as a celibate vegetarian he'd live a thousand years. Well, he was on the right lines with the vegetarianism but completely wrong about the sex. Since ancient times, the Chinese have equated the retention of *ching* (male sexual energy) with longevity. But the ancient Chinese also devised a way of making love without losing *ching*. It's described below. Poor Chen Dong obviously didn't know about it.

The normal developments of ageing

As we get older our way of having sex changes. That's inevitable. But it certainly doesn't have to be a change for the worse. In fact, very many older couples who continue to enjoy active sex lives say it's *better* than before. They wouldn't go back. For healthy couples, the fifties and sixties are years of wonderful sexual compatibility. And many couples continue to be sexually active through their seventies and well into their eighties.

Just look at all the advantages of being older:

▶ *more time for sex*
▶ *more knowledge about sex*
▶ *more skill in sex*
▶ *more experimentation in sex*
▶ *more knowledge of your own body*
▶ *more knowledge of your partner's body (assuming you've been together a while)*
▶ *more multi-orgasmic*
▶ *more control over ejaculation*
▶ *less guilt about sex*
▶ *less inhibition about sex*
▶ *no fear of pregnancy*
▶ *no periods*
▶ *no worries about the side effects of contraceptives*
▶ *less likelihood of premature ejaculation.*

So sex can get better and better, if you have the right attitude and approach. The important thing is to *be forewarned about normal, inevitable, age-related evolution and work with it.*

If the changes in your body take you by surprise, you may imagine there's something wrong with you and be put off sex, or even worry yourself into impotence. So here, first of all, are some of the normal age-related developments in a man.

Don't panic if:

▶ *your penis takes longer to get erect and longer still to become fully rigid*
▶ *more stimulation is required to cause erection*
▶ *there's a loss of sex drive for a time following unusual physical effort*

- *you have fewer ejaculatory contractions*
- *the power of the contractions diminishes*
- *your penis goes down very quickly after ejaculation*
- *the refractory period (the period during which, after ejaculation, it isn't possible to have sex) gets longer and longer.*

Insight

All of these are normal developments. The first two need not cause any problems in lovemaking. As regards the third, just don't expect to make love following extreme exertion. All the others can be dealt with very happily by adopting new styles of lovemaking, involving the Tao and multiple male orgasms (which we'll look at later on).

If you're a woman, don't panic if:

- *your breasts, labia and clitoris don't enlarge as much as they used to during sex*
- *the number of orgasmic contractions diminishes*
- *your vagina takes longer to become lubricated*
- *you experience a burning sensation when peeing for a day or two after sex.*

Insight

Again, these are all normal developments which can be dealt with. Don't let them cause you to have sex less often. That will only accelerate the changes. Keep up regular sex but use plenty of artificial lubricant. Not only will it make penetration just as pleasurable as when you were young but it will protect you from the burning sensation.

Note, however, that the following things are *not* normal:

- *Pain during penetration, even with artificial lubricant.*
- *Painful contractions of the uterus during orgasm.*

If you experience these problems, seek medical attention.

Managing the effects of ageing

Some people think you shouldn't do anything about the effects of ageing when it comes to sex. That a woman should simply stop at the menopause and a man should stop when he's no longer a stud. Germaine Greer has written that a woman might prefer to 'opt out' of sex at the menopause if her partner 'takes a good deal longer about it' than he used to. But, for both women and men, taking a good deal longer can add enormously to the pleasure. And the emotional, intellectual and spiritual aspects of sex carry on regardless.

FREQUENCY

The most important sexual tonic is sex itself. The more you do it, the more you'll be able to do it. Studies have compared older women who had sex at least once a week with older women who had sex only occasionally. The women who had regular sex were still able to enjoy four to seven contractions of the vagina at orgasm, compared with three to five for the other women. They showed much higher levels of myotonia (the muscular tension that builds up and is released in orgasm) and were more likely to experience contraction of the rectal sphincter, which is rare after 50. Contractions of the uterus were also more likely. The opening of the outer labia, vasocongestion of the inner labia, sexual flush, breast enlargement, nipple erection and – above all – enlargement of the clitoris were all more apparent in women who had regular sex lives. Interestingly, in a Masters and Johnson study, two women aged 61–70 and one aged 73 all had the lubrication speed of young women. *These were the only women to have continued sex at a level of once or twice a week.*

What's more, regular sex is a natural form of hormone replacement therapy, because it boosts various hormones including oestrogen. A woman who continues a high level of sexual activity is less likely to have problems both during and after the menopause.

As for men, the position is similar. Frequent sex causes older men's testosterone levels to rise. It also makes the penis function more assuredly.

> ## Insight
>
> How frequent is frequent? Well, you should certainly aim to have some kind of sex (not necessarily intercourse) every day. Why not? If it's nice *and* beneficial it makes sense to do it as often as possible. And if, for whatever reason, you're not able to have sex with a partner, it's important to continue to enjoy solo sex.

STRENGTHENING THE PC MUSCLE

Both men and women have a group of muscles popularly known as the 'PC muscle' running from the pubic bone to the spine. (Strictly speaking, the PC or pubococcygeus is just one of the group but I'll use the term here in its popular sense.) In a man, the PC muscle passes under the prostate gland. In a woman, it supports the internal sexual apparatus. When a man flexes his PC muscle, his erect penis twitches rather pleasantly inside the vagina. And when a woman flexes hers, her vagina strokes the penis. What's more, in both sexes, the stronger the PC muscle the stronger the orgasm.

Unfortunately, the PC muscle can become slack over the years, meaning not only less exciting sex but also a tendency to let dribbles of urine escape. So it's a good idea to exercise the PC muscle regularly. You probably already know which one it is, but if not it's the one you can squeeze to cut off the flow of urine when peeing.

A basic exercise is to contract the muscle. You can flex it quite invisibly which means you can do the exercise anywhere – sitting on the train, at a desk or watching the TV. But you do need to concentrate and contract the muscle as hard as you can for at least six seconds, which means a strange, tense look may appear on your face. Repeat five times with a couple of seconds rest between each contraction. That makes one set. Do three sets a day.

Unfortunately, it's very hard to build up a muscle if it doesn't have a resistance to work against. Which, of course, is why people lift weights. Women have an advantage here because they have vaginas into which resistance can be inserted. One style is, indeed, a dumbbell especially designed for the vagina. Another style is the famous Kegel device, invented by Dr Arnold Kegel in 1947. In essence it's like a large clothes peg which you have to squeeze using the walls of your vagina. If you choose that design, select a model with a variable resistance which can be increased as your PC muscle grows stronger.

VIBRATORS

By age 50, a vibrator or two (or three) is a vital piece of equipment. A vibrator applied on or close to the clitoris prior to intercourse speeds lubrication. In fact, giving yourself an orgasm with a vibrator is a very practical and enjoyable prelude to sex with your partner. As for a man, a vibrator applied to the penis can increase stiffness. And there are all kinds of ways you can use vibrators to increase arousal and pleasure generally.

If you already use a vibrator and don't seem to get the stimulation that you used to, consider switching to a more powerful design. Rigid mains-powered models give the strongest sensations and some of them can be used *all over* your body, which is very nice.

You can buy vibrators in a sex shop or on the internet.

LUBRICATION

Artificial lubricants are little short of miraculous. They completely take away the discomfort older women can feel on penetration and restore the pleasure for both of you.

If you're a woman aged around 60, for example, you'll be slower to lubricate (one to three minutes on average compared to 10–30 seconds when you were 20) and the quantity will be less. What's more, as you get older so the walls of the vagina become thinner and, as a result, the urethra (which runs along the wall of the vagina) gets irritated when you have sex. If you feel a burning sensation on peeing for a day or two afterwards this (rather than cystitis) could be the cause. This is one of the reasons extra lubrication is so important because it, as it were, insulates your urethra.

Don't for a moment feel embarrassed about the idea of needing additional lubrication. In fact, almost all couples can benefit from it, especially during long sessions. Your man will be experiencing age-related changes of his own. So don't give it a second thought.

In terms of pleasure, both men and women gain enormously from the use of a lubricant. If you need to be convinced, compare the effect of running your fingers over your own skin, firstly when it's dry and secondly when it's been lubricated with a few drops of oil from the kitchen. The difference is amazing and all the more so as you get older – sex without it is like running an engine without oil.

So if you've been relying on saliva, now is the time to treat yourself to the best lubricant for you. The main kinds are:

▶ **Water-based lubricants.** *These feel very natural. Their only disadvantage is that they dry fairly quickly and need frequent renewal.*
▶ **Oil-based lubricants.** *These last longer than water-based lubricants but shouldn't be used with condoms.*
▶ Silicone lubricants. *These are extremely long-lasting but some couples don't like them because, although they're slippery, they don't actually feel wet.*

There are literally dozens of different brands, some thin, some thick, some perfumed, some not, and some with additives designed to enhance arousal. Have fun trying them out. The number one rule is to use plenty – on the penis, on the vaginal lips, inside the vagina and around the anus, if you like anal stimulation. For a good selection you'll need to go to a sex shop or buy online.

EROTICA

Malcolm Muggeridge wrote that pornography's aim of exciting sexual desire was 'unnecessary in the case of the young, inconvenient in the case of the middle-aged and unseemly in the old'. Wittily expressed, but wrong on every count.

Erotica can be used by both women and men to help maintain sexual function. Men tend to favour visual images, as do a growing number of women. Many other women favour the written word. Used regularly, erotica can give your sex hormones a boost. Used before lovemaking, erotica can increase arousal.

If you're a woman who's been shocked to discover your man using pornography, try not to be. It's perfectly normal for men and it's no reflection on you. On the contrary, your man may be doing his best to maintain his sexual function so that he *can* make love to you. Older men sometimes avoid sex because they're not confident they can get an erection; masturbating to a sexy photograph or DVD (but not to ejaculation) is a way of checking that an erection is possible.

However, pornography can be a problem if your man is:

▶ *addicted*
▶ *seeking out increasingly bizarre sex acts*
▶ *prefers it to real sex with you*
▶ *wants you to copy things that you're very much against.*

If you feel there's a problem, try to discuss it calmly, putting your own point of view and giving proper consideration to his.

Men's problems

IMPOTENCE

Many older men believe themselves to be impotent when they're not at all. If a man can masturbate successfully, he can have sex successfully. It's as simple as that. If that's you, or your partner, then clearly the problem is psychological. Nevertheless, it still has to be overcome.

When a man is young, the very sight of his partner naked is enough to cause an erection. But sometime in middle age those automatic erections occasionally stop. A quick, discreet fumble under the bedclothes usually puts things right. Then, one day, a lot more than a quick rub becomes necessary. The man panics. And that's it. From then on, sex is anticipated with a feeling of stress. And stress is the enemy of erections.

If that sounds like your kind of 'impotence' the solution is fairly simple.

The first thing you need to do is maximize your oxytocin which, as we've seen, is a hormone that increases the sensitivity of your skin, including, of course, your penis. Your oxytocin level goes up every time you touch your partner, so the way to maximize it is to give her a massage. Use massage cream or oil, preferably scented with something arousing (such as sandalwood). Concentrate. Don't be perfunctory. Really *feel* her contours with your hands and take your time. Remember, you're not only giving your partner pleasure, you're increasing your own responsiveness.

Secondly, it's vitally important that you feel free to masturbate in front of your partner – and that your partner feels free to masturbate in front of you. There's absolutely no need for either of you to feel threatened or humiliated. It's a fact of life that we all have the ability to excite ourselves in ways that our partners can't. There's no reason we can't incorporate that into lovemaking with a partner. Once that's accepted, then a lot of the stress evaporates.

So if 'foreplay', including massage, doesn't do the trick, then masturbate – and ask your partner to masturbate at the same time, so you can watch her. Most men find that very exciting.

Helping a man who is 'impotent'

Stress is the enemy of erections, which means that fear of impotence is self-fulfilling. The first rule, then, is that if your man fails to have a sufficient erection you must be completely relaxed about it. Don't do or say anything he might interpret as disappointment, embarrassment or some kind of reproach. Be casual. Say how much you'd like it if, instead, he pleasured you with his tongue and fingers. As he does so, communicate your excitement with plenty of moans and groans. Removing the pressure to perform while simultaneously increasing the heat may be all that's necessary.

It's vital that your man should feel completely free to masturbate in front of you. If he feels relaxed doing that, a lot of anxiety will disappear. Ask if he'd like to watch you masturbate. Most men find it highly exciting. Then suggest he masturbates at the same time. Make masturbation a completely normal part of lovemaking.

APHRODISIACS FOR MEN

In middle age, it's normal for men to start thinking about ways of maintaining their performance. But before you start looking for 'chemical' solutions it might be as well to review your lifestyle. The enemies of testosterone and sex include:

- ▶ *alcohol (but see the insight below)*
- ▶ *tobacco*
- ▶ *a high fat intake*
- ▶ *a paunch*
- ▶ *lack of exercise.*

See if there are any improvements you can make in those areas.

Insight

Grape skins *may* contain resveratrol (see page 75) which has been shown to increase testosterone. Drinking red wine (the production of which involves the greatest contact with the skins) *could* therefore boost the hormone. However, given the negative effects of alcohol, it would be better to take a resveratrol supplement.

You might also like to consider the following food supplements:

- ▶ Nettle root – *inhibits aromatase which, especially in men carrying a lot of fat, converts testosterone to the 'female' hormone oestrogen.*
- ▶ Saw Palmetto – *helps to inhibit a chemical called sex hormone binding globulin (SHBG) which effectively 'ties up' testosterone in the body; the result is an increase in the all-important 'free' testosterone. It also inhibits enlargement of the prostate gland with age.*
- ▶ Zinc – *if you're deficient, as many men are, then a supplement will perk you up. About 15 mg a day is about right for most men.*
- ▶ Korean red ginseng, L-Arginine and the hormone DHEA *have all been scientifically proven to have at least some benefit in certain circumstances.*

▶ Cistanchis, Cynomorium songaricum, Damiana, Epimedium sagittatum *(horny goat weed)*, Eurycoma longfolia, Maca, Mucuna pruriens, Muira puama *and* Tribulus terrestris. *There is plenty of anecdotal evidence that these (and others, too) are effective in various degrees.*

Remember, there are not the controls over food supplements that there are for medicines. Supplements sent for analysis often don't contain the claimed ingredients and sometimes contain toxins. Only buy from the most reputable sources you can find.

If you prefer not to take 'drugs' then a type of magnet therapy called Pulsed Electromagnetic Field Therapy (PEMF) may be for you. You have to wear a little box containing the apparatus close to the genitals. In one double-blind, placebo-controlled trial, 80 per cent of men reported significant improvement after three weeks.

Insight

If the problem seems to be serious and long term then you should seek professional advice. Viagra is only the most famous of a whole range of treatments that are now available and you need a professional to decide what's right for you. Don't self-medicate with prescription drugs from the internet; they should *only* be prescribed by a doctor after a medical check-up.

Women's problems

FEMALE SEXUAL AROUSAL DISORDER

A great deal of rubbish has been written about female sexual arousal disorder (FSAD). Some doctors in the USA are saying that about 45 per cent of women suffer from FSAD, which is absurd. What they really mean is that 45 per cent of women aren't behaving the way men would like them to. That's not the same thing at all.

If *you* think there's something wrong with you, if *you* think your response isn't what it used to, if *you're* not happy, if you have a *specific* problem, then, of course, seek a solution. But it's worth taking note of the feminists who say that *not* feeling desire for a dishevelled, unwashed, overweight and sexually incompetent companion is hardly a disorder. It's a good point. At least in some cases, FSAD might really be MUD – male unattractiveness disorder.

In general, women could be said to be sexually neutral. Unlike men, they usually need a good reason to feel aroused. So, guys, if your partner seems to you to be suffering from FSAD, just ask yourself if the problem doesn't lie with *you* rather than her.

Insight

It's easy to get out of the habit of having sex when there are health or other problems in your life. If that's your case, remember that it's also easy to get back into the habit. Make the decision to restart regular sex and your body will respond by producing more sex hormones. Very soon you'll be *wanting* sex again.

THE MENOPAUSE

For some women, the menopause is an extremely difficult time, while others hardly notice it at all. There's good evidence that continuing an active sex life throughout the menopause reduces the severity of symptoms. Why should that be? Because, as we've seen, sexual activity tends to elevate the level of certain hormones, especially oestrogen, which otherwise would fall very rapidly. With continued sexual activity, the decline is much slower and the body adjusts far more easily.

What's more, women often enjoy sex more after the menopause. One theory is that while women's oestrogen levels fall at menopause, their testosterone levels don't fall so much (women have testosterone, too, remember?). Just as with men, testosterone plays a role in a woman's sex drive and when it isn't 'counterbalanced' by so much oestrogen, the libido goes up. In addition, 30 or more years of sexual activity will have increased the system of veins in the genitals, leading to easier orgasms. An older woman is also more skilful and has thrown her inhibitions out of the bedroom window.

Menopause removes the fear of pregnancy and eliminates the need for contraception. If male condoms have been the choice of contraceptive for the last fertile years, then a man is going to notice a substantial increase in stimulation and a woman is going to notice a warmer feeling, increased sensitivity, a contribution to lubrication from him and no more of that funny squeaky sound. Nor is there any longer the need for him to withdraw immediately after ejaculation (in case the condom slips off) so she can enjoy the feeling of fullness and contact for longer.

A woman can also help maintain her oestrogen levels by eating certain foods, particularly soy products (see page 31), flaxseed (linseed), alfalfa and mung beans, because they're all high in oestrogen-like substances known as phyto-oestrogens. It's certainly worth trying herbal remedies, too (highly rated by many women). There's anecdotal evidence for *Damiana*, *Maca*, *Muira puama* and *Tribulus terrestris*.

If regular sex, soy and herbs aren't enough, you may like to consider hormone replacement therapy (HRT), which directly boosts oestrogen. Many women are very happy with HRT but there is an increased risk of breast cancer. How significant is it? For postmenopausal women aged 50–65:

▶ *of those not on HRT around 32 in 1,000 will get breast cancer*
▶ *of those on oestrogen-only HRT for ten years, around 37 in 1,000 will get breast cancer*
▶ *of those on oestrogen-progestogen HRT for ten years, around 51 in 1,000 will get breast cancer.*

The *increase* in risk, then, is significant for oestrogen-progestogen HRT but the *overall* risk is still fairly small, and all the more so if HRT is only used for a year or two. The reason for adding progestogen to some forms of HRT is that it protects against cancer of the uterus. Another type of HRT increases testosterone. So this is a complicated subject and the decision about whether or not to try HRT, and if so which form, is one you can only take in conjunction with a qualified professional.

> ### Insight
> Many couples use alcohol as a way of overcoming inhibitions but by middle age you shouldn't have any inhibitions left. In fact, alcohol *reduces* physical responsiveness and the effect on your sex life is much worse when you're older. Too much alcohol will considerably decrease a man's erections and reduce sensation in the clitoris and vagina. So don't have more than a few sips before sex.

A NEW WAY OF HAVING SEX

The older years can be the time of greatest sexual compatibility. As a man's drive for ejaculation diminishes, so a woman's drive for orgasm often increases with the result that the two meet on the common ground of a whole body experience with plenty of cuddling and tenderness.

TAO

In many cultures, ejaculation wasn't seen as the high point of sex. It was seen as a failure on the part of a man. A mistake. An error. It meant the pleasures of lovemaking were abruptly ended. It meant, perhaps, giving up an hour of delight in return for sensations that, however pleasurable, lasted only a few seconds.

So if you're a man who can't ejaculate as much as you used to, or if you have a partner who can't, don't worry about it. It's not a disadvantage at all. On the contrary it's a considerable advantage. It means you can *enjoy lovemaking as often as you want but without ejaculation.*

Possibly nowhere was this philosophy more developed than in the Chinese spiritual tradition of the Tao. The Taoists believed that men should preserve their 'ching', because when a man ejaculated he lost not just semen but his entire vitality, his physical, mental and spiritual energy. That's why, when older men ejaculate, they often feel a bit 'flat' for a day or so afterwards.

It would seem your ability to ejaculate when you're older is related to your ability when you were younger. Shere Hite, the sexologist, took data from a man who was still ejaculating five or six times a week at age 64. But that was as compared with some 40 ejaculations a week at age 16. The man was something of an exception, of course, but the drop of 85 per cent in sexual performance probably holds good for most men. In other words, if you used to ejaculate once a day in your teens you'll probably be ejaculating once a week by the time you retire.

Sun S'sû-Mo, a Taoist physician born in 581 CE, set down the wisdom of the Taoist tradition when he recommended the following frequencies for ejaculation:

▶ *age 20 – once every four days*
▶ *age 30 – once every eight days*
▶ *age 40 – once every ten days*
▶ *age 50 – once every 20 days*
▶ *age 60 – once every 30 days.*

In Taoist thought, the seasons also played a role in ejaculation frequency. Basically, a man could have the most ejaculations in the spring, rather fewer in the summer and none at all in winter.

In practice it means this. What seemed to be a disadvantage becomes an advantage. If you're a man, then, when making love, don't even try to ejaculate. Simply maintain a level of excitement slightly below the climax level. If you're a woman, don't expect your man to ejaculate.

If, as a man, you're not convinced that sex without ejaculation is going to be enjoyable just ask yourself this: *What are the things that I enjoy about sex?*

Let me make some suggestions. Undressing your partner. Inhaling the perfume of her skin. The physical comfort of your naked bodies hugged together. Exciting your partner. Feeling her body tremble in your arms as she has her first orgasm. Feeling your own excitement rise. Giving yourself up to the rapture as the dopamine hits your brain. I could go on. My point is this. When you feel you can ejaculate, then ejaculate if you wish. But when you have the feeling you won't be able to, why not still enjoy all the other marvellous things about lovemaking? You're not losing anything. You're gaining extra lovemaking sessions.

Some writers claim you can have intercourse several times a day by following the Tao. That's not actually true for an older man. In reality, even though you don't ejaculate, you'll still lose a little fluid. And even if you don't orgasm, various mechanisms in the brain and elsewhere will get fatigued. But it is true that you can probably have sex every day. You won't have any fears over performance and, as a result of that, your performance will probably improve.

Insight

After the age of about 60, you may find that if you let your erection go down you can't get it up again, *even though you haven't ejaculated*. If this is happening to you, the key is not to get erect until you're both ready for intercourse. In other words, concentrate on your partner and don't let her stimulate you. Just before intercourse, stimulate yourself or let your partner stimulate you with her mouth and fingers, insert immediately and maintain a steady level of excitement. If your erection isn't strong enough to penetrate your partner even with lots of stimulation, try encircling your penis with your forefinger and thumb to stiffen the tip and maintain the 'ring' while you move your glans round and round and in and out.

Multiple orgasms for men

You can increase the excitement of the basic Taoist sexual technique by learning how, even though you don't ejaculate, *you can still experience orgasm*. In fact, a whole string of orgasms.

You may be puzzled by this if you think that orgasm and ejaculation are one and the same thing. But, in fact, they're not. Orgasm is the muscular contraction, while ejaculation is the passage of the semen.

▶ *It's possible to ejaculate without having an orgasm.*
▶ *It's possible to orgasm without ejaculating.*

In reality, orgasm without ejaculation feels very different. Some sexologists call these kinds of orgasms *contractile-phase orgasms* or *pelvic orgasms*. I prefer to call them *partial orgasms*, because that's what they are. Nevertheless, once you get good at the technique, you'll find that each of these partial orgasms is more powerful than the previous one. Eventually you'll reach a state of ecstasy, far beyond the normal sexual experience. Here's a list of some of the advantages of multiple orgasms:

▶ *You'll never be afraid of not being able to perform.*
▶ *You and your partner can enjoy sex for longer.*
▶ *Because lovemaking lasts longer, your partner will enjoy multiple orgasms as well.*
▶ *You won't lose your sexual vitality in the way you do with 'ordinary' sex.*
▶ *You and your partner can have sex more often – once a day, for example, or even several times a day.*
▶ *After a session of multiple orgasms you won't have the flat feeling you do with ejaculation.*
▶ *Your hormone balance will be different – you'll feel more affectionate and loving.*
▶ *You'll feel 'mystical'.*

Different sexologists describe different methods for stopping ejaculation and achieving multiple male orgasms. One involves strengthening the PC muscle (see page 224) until it can actually shut off the ejaculation. Another involves pressing a place between the testicles and the anus, known as the Million Dollar Point. And there are still others.

The technique I'm going to describe here is the most straightforward.

Probably you already use Stop/Go as a way of prolonging your pleasure. That simply means that you cease stimulation once you get 'too' excited, let your erection subside a little, then begin again. But when you do that you probably don't experience a partial orgasm. For that to happen, you need to refine that technique so you can get closer and closer to the point of no return without 'going over the edge' into ejaculation.

It's simple in principle, but it's not easy in practice because in order to experience orgasm without ejaculation you have to get very, very close indeed. So, while you're experimenting things are often going to 'go wrong.' Never mind. Enjoy your mistakes when they happen.

You're going to have to let your partner know what you're planning because her co-operation is essential to success. When you need to *stop* it's no good if she continues to *go*. She has to cease stimulation as well.

In fact, the first time you try this with your partner it may not be hugely enjoyable for either of you. You're going to have to concentrate hard on what you're doing and that means taking attention away from her. And if your partner is trying to help you, she, too, will be concentrating on your starting and stopping so as not to tip you over into ejaculation. Rather than have more orgasms, she may at first have fewer. But don't give up after just one or two less than mind-blowing sessions. You need to give it, say, a month before you decide whether it's something you want to do regularly, occasionally or not at all. With practice you'll find you can control yourself with less effort and your partner will find she can once again relax into her own orgasms.

Insight

The technique won't work if you say you'll 'see how you feel' when the moment comes. You must be adamant in your own mind. When you get close to the level of excitement at which the multiple orgasms occur, switch to a position that puts you in control of the movement (if you're not in one already).

As soon as you start to experience a partial orgasm:

▶ *stop all movement*
▶ *stop tensing your muscles*
▶ *stop all 'dirty talk'*
▶ *stop all fantasizing*
▶ *stop looking at your partner's body*
▶ *stop revelling in the sensual feelings*
▶ *stop all stimulation of every kind.*

And, most important of all:

▶ *pull your stomach sharply in towards your back and envisage the energy from your genitals being sucked up your spine into your brain. Some men find it helps to pant, others prefer not to breathe at all for a few moments. Rolling your eyes up can also help.*

Insight

Eastern thought holds that you can divert energy from your genitals by taking your partner's tongue into your mouth and sucking it. Western thought would be that you've simply diverted attention somewhere else. Whichever is right, the technique does work as a way of cooling off a little bit when you feel you're in danger of going past the point of no return.

A lifetime of sex with the same partner

Is it possible to keep sex exciting right through a relationship that might last for 60 years or more? It certainly is. The secret is to keep fit for sex (see Chapters 2–4) and to keep finding new things to do. Buy sex books from time to time and look for some fresh techniques. As long as you have the creative impulse and creative ideas you'll never be bored.

Remember, you're not only having sex with a physical presence, you're also having sex with a soul. Even if you don't literally believe that you should at least reflect that the beauty of the inner person is by far the most important thing.

The comments of couples in their seventies and eighties about their sex lives are not only cause for optimism but are also deeply moving. A man in his seventies having intercourse four or five times a week with a new partner, also in her seventies, who 'almost always has an orgasm'. A couple in their eighties who relish an hour of 'sex play' in the morning, a two hour siesta 'naked in each other's arms' and another half hour or so of sex at night because every day is 'precious'. And the 82-year-old man who said the greatest pleasure in sex was the feeling of 'oneness' with his wife.

10 THINGS TO REMEMBER

1 *An active sex life can take four to seven years off your appearance and add anything up to ten years to your life.*

2 *Sex can get better after 50 for both women and men; for women, the ratio of testosterone to oestrogen normally increases, thus boosting sex drive.*

3 *The best exercise for sex is sex itself, but you should both also make a point of exercising your PC muscles every day.*

4 *Every couple over 50 should have at least one vibrator and plenty of artificial lubricant.*

5 *Erotica is a good way of boosting sex drive; men over 50 should use erotica and masturbation without ejaculation to boost their testosterone levels.*

6 *Many men who think they're impotent are simply suffering from anxiety about normal changes in sexual response.*

7 *You should feel free to masturbate in front of one another.*

8 *Exercise and food supplements can help overcome low sex drive; prescription drugs for impotence should only be obtained from a doctor following a proper examination.*

9 *Regular sex is itself a form of hormone replacement therapy (HRT) and can ease the symptoms of the menopause; soy products and other foods containing phyto-oestrogens can also help.*

10 *Age is no barrier to great sex. Men over 50 can still have sex every day by following the Tao or using the technique for multiple orgasms, and as long as you both keep fit you can still enjoy sex in your seventies and eighties.*

HOW MUCH LONGER ARE YOU GOING TO LIVE NOW?

▶ *Are you aware of the normal developments of ageing and have you adapted your sexual techniques accordingly?*
▶ *Are you having sex frequently?*
▶ *Are you doing your PC muscle exercises every day?*
▶ *Do you have at least one vibrator?*
▶ *Are you using artificial lubricant?*
▶ *Are you using erotica for extra stimulation, especially while masturbating?*
▶ *Are you keeping fit, slim and flexible?*
▶ *Are you a non-smoker and very moderate drinker?*
▶ *Are you exploring non-ejaculatory sex?*
▶ *Are you still thinking up new things to do in bed?*

Score:

If you answered 'yes' to seven or more questions you're obviously still enjoying your sex life and that's very important for longevity. Move on to the next chapter.

If you answered 'yes' to between four and six questions you're on the right lines but there's quite a bit more you could do to ensure you go on enjoying great sex for many more years. You can also move on to the next chapter but re-read this one from time to time with the aim of eventually putting everything into practice.

If you answered 'yes' to three or fewer questions and you're over 50, then you need to do a lot more if you want to continue enjoying sex, together with its physical and mental health benefits, into old age. Possibly you're still inhibited about sex and find it hard to discuss physical changes with your partner. If so, that's something you need to deal with. Possibly you just assumed that your sex life would go into decline after 50 and are doing nothing about it, but it certainly doesn't have to be that way. Read the chapter again, put as much as possible into effect, and don't read on until you score at least four 'yesses'. Sex is a big subject and you might also like to read *Teach Yourself: Have Great Sex*.

11

....

Spirituality

In this chapter you will learn:
- *how spirituality increases longevity*
- *how you can be spiritual even if you don't believe in God or follow any religion.*

Every culture in every age has had its religious beliefs. Some of those religions have had gods, some have had a god, and some have effectively had no god. But they've all believed in *something* intangible. Something beyond. And while that doesn't prove the existence of anything whatsoever, it does prove a human yearning for such kinds of beliefs. If you're absolutely free of those kinds of feelings then this chapter can do nothing to improve your longevity. But, in that case, you're a very rare person.

In this book so far we've looked at a number of *practical* measures you can take to improve your chances of living longer, as well as a few that are a little less tangible. But all of them have had an obvious logic. It's not difficult to see how eating the right foods and taking proper exercise can keep a 'machine' like the body functioning correctly. Nor should it be surprising that love and companionship are essential for physical and mental health.

But what about religion and spirituality? Whatever else may come from following a particular religion or spiritual feeling, is there any evidence at all that longevity will be increased?

In fact, there's quite a lot.

A nine-year study of 21,000 Americans published in 1999 concluded that:

- ▶ *people who attended religious services once a week or less had a 20 per cent higher rate of mortality than those who attended more than once a week.*
- ▶ *people who never attended religious services had a 50 per cent higher rate of mortality than those who attended the most frequently.*
- ▶ *people who never attended religious services had a 400 per cent higher rate of mortality specifically from infectious diseases, respiratory diseases and diabetes than those who attended the most frequently.*

A 16-year study in Israel found lower rates of premature death in religious kibbutzim (collective agricultural settlements) as compared with secular kibbutzim.

A review of 42 separate studies collectively involving nearly 126,000 Americans and published in 2000 concluded that active religious involvement increased the chance of living longer by 29 per cent.

What does that actually mean in terms of years? Several studies, including one by the University of Pittsburgh Medical Center, have measured the more tangible aspects of spirituality and concluded that people who attend religious services every week live two to three years longer than people who seldom or never go.

These findings need to be interpreted with caution. After all, committed religious people are, on average, perhaps less likely to indulge in risky behaviour than others. They're probably less likely to become involved with drugs, for example, less likely to abuse alcohol, less likely to indulge in casual sex, more likely to commit themselves to a relationship, more likely to take care of themselves and, by the very nature of religious attendance, are socially connected. We know these are all factors that promote longevity.

But is there anything to say that religious or spiritual belief itself is conducive to a longer life? Yes, there is. At least four studies have concluded that even when the practical and social benefits of religious attendance are allowed for, there's still a small but important 'spiritual component' that contributes to longevity.

In that case, what exactly is it and how does it work?

There are a number of possible mechanisms. In general it can be said that religious and spiritual beliefs:

▶ *promote gratitude and acceptance*
▶ *promote optimism and positive thoughts*
▶ *reduce stress and enhance the ability to cope with emotional distress*
▶ *reduce the likelihood of depression and suicide*
▶ *improve the ability to cope with illness and surgery*
▶ *improve the ability to cope with death*
▶ *give life a point.*

Let's look at some of these.

Gratitude and acceptance

Most religions teach thankfulness and among the non-religious, too, it's an innate part of a spiritual outlook. The *Book of Common Prayer*, for example, asks: 'Give us grateful hearts', while a standard Christian phrase is: 'May the Lord make us truly thankful'.

A North American Indian tells how, in his family, the custom is to smudge both the food and the diners with sage smoke, to thank both the Great Spirit and the Earth Mother and then to add: 'May the wholesomeness of the food before us bring out the wholeness of the Spirit within us.'

An old Scottish grace goes like this: 'Some hae meat and cannae eat, some would eat that want it, but we hae meat and we can eat, sae let the Lord be thankit.'

To the non-religious, saying grace may seem pointless, dated and even corny but there's an important philosophical point here that applies to everybody. Expressing the sentiment in different words, it's partly and quite simply about appreciating food, appreciating everything that grows on the Earth, appreciating life itself and, indeed, *relishing your own life*. Making the most out of it. And, surely, no one could quarrel with that. That, in turn, fosters optimism.

Insight

Nowadays we're all too likely to worry about material things, about houses and cars and other possessions, about keeping up with the Joneses and, specifically, about *money*. So it's important to remind ourselves from time to time that there are other, more important things in life we can all enjoy.

Optimism

Optimists live longer than pessimists. That's a fact established by the Psychiatric Centre GGZ Delfland in the Netherlands. In 1995, a team led by Erik Giltay asked 999 men and women aged from 65 to 85 to complete a questionnaire about their morale, self-respect and degree of optimism. Nine years later, 397 of the group had died. And here's the interesting thing: among the optimists the number of deaths, specifically from heart failure, was 23 per cent lower than for the pessimists.

But there was even better news for optimists: the risk of death among optimists from all causes was an astonishing 55 per cent lower than for pessimists.

Why should this be? It seems that pessimistic people are more likely to be stressed, to suffer from high blood pressure, to turn to alcohol, tobacco and comfort-eating and, not surprisingly, to develop serious depression.

Clearly, strong religious beliefs tend to promote optimism. If you believe you and all those you love will be reunited in an afterlife, you have little to fear. If you don't believe in an afterlife but nevertheless have strong spiritual feelings, they, too, provide a cushion against life's problems.

It's true that in some cases strong religious feelings can have the opposite effect, causing people to feel guilty and even to fear punishment in a life to come. In fact, a Harris survey in 2007 found that 62 per cent of Americans did, indeed, believe in the Devil and in the existence of Hell. If you do have such fears, I'm sure they're groundless. It seems very unlikely that a God who created a universe that stretches over billions of light years, contains literally billions of stars and attendant planets, and possibly thousands of billions of human-like beings, would be petty. You've done many good things in your life and you will do more. That's what counts.

Insight

In one study it was found that optimism in youth was associated with *higher* mortality. The reason seems to be that optimistic young people are more cavalier about smoking and drinking and take greater risks. So there's a caveat. Be optimistic but don't let your optimism lead you into doing dangerous things.

Coping skills

We all have difficult, sad and tragic things happen in our lives from time to time. And we have to cope with them so we can get through to a point where, one day, we can enjoy life to the full again. Different people have different ways of coping but religious and spiritual beliefs can certainly be enormously helpful. In a nine-year study of 1,000 men, seriously ill in hospital, those with powerful religious convictions were far less likely to be depressed. Around a fifth said it was only religion that was keeping them going. It has to be said that, in these extreme circumstances, believers didn't have longer survival rates than non-believers, but the quality of their final days seems to have been better on average.

Giving life a point

Many people, probably most people, feel the need for their lives to have some kind of point. It comes up again and again in surveys. The notion that life might be utterly futile is something the human psyche seems to find difficult to bear. That doesn't prove things one way or the other, of course, but it does mean that people who believe they have a role in the grand order of things, or a specific task for which they've somehow been chosen, or a guaranteed place in an afterlife, enjoy a sense of purpose and, as a result, a greater degree of tranquillity.

Choosing what to believe

You can choose what food to eat and how much exercise to take. But you can't choose to believe in a religion or philosophy on the grounds that you may live two years longer. Either you believe something is true or you don't. With something like that, you can pretend to others but you can't pretend to yourself.

There are, however, certain things to do with religion and spirituality about which you *can* make a conscious decision:

> ▶ *If you consider yourself to be a member of a certain faith but don't attend religious services, you could make a conscious decision to start attending regularly. Why not begin this week? It's the logical thing to do. It accords with your beliefs and by attending you'll be gaining various social benefits.*

- ▸ *If you're not a member of any religious faith purely because you've never given much thought to the subject, why not take the time to investigate various religions to see what they have to say. You might be surprised.*
- ▸ *If you're quite certain you could never follow any of the world's religions, you can still make a decision to explore and develop your own spirituality. There's no contradiction, as we'll see in a moment.*

Prayer

Most religions incorporate some form of prayer. It's part of the practice of Buddhism, Christianity, Christian Science, Hinduism, Islam, Judaism, Shinto and others. Sometimes prayers are silent, sometimes out loud, sometimes they involve swaying, dancing or whirling, sometimes stillness.

The purpose of prayer also varies. Among other things, it could be to:

- ▸ *ask for help in a difficult situation*
- ▸ *ask for help on behalf of others*
- ▸ *become more in tune with things beyond the material world*
- ▸ *experience the spiritual realm.*

Prayers are often used to seek help for someone else in difficulty, but is there any evidence that they work? Although some studies do claim to have found a positive effect, the answer is no. All of those studies have suffered from flaws of some kind, usually because they weren't genuinely double-blind (that's to say, with no one knowing who was being prayed for and who wasn't).

One of the first 'anti-prayer' studies was carried out by Francis Galton in 1872. He reasoned that if prayers were effective then members of the British royal family should live longer than anybody else, since millions of people prayed for them every

Sunday. After examining the statistics he concluded that members of the royal family didn't live longer than the general population and that prayers therefore didn't work. Not the most scientific study, but there have been many better ones since.

One of the most authoritative double-blind studies was conducted by the Mayo Clinic in 2001. It found no significant difference in the recovery rates of patients who were being prayed for when compared with the others. A similar study by Duke University came to the same conclusion.

Not all religious people, anyway, would claim that prayer could be used in such a manner. Some cite Deuteronomy: 'You shall not test the Lord thy God.'

But none of this means that prayer has no purpose at all. For a start, when patients *know* they're being prayed for (which in double-blind trials they don't, of course) many do show an improvement in morale and faster recovery. A study by CentraState, a not-for-profit health organization in New Jersey, concluded that knowing you're being prayed for 'may help reduce stress and anxiety, promote a more positive outlook, and strengthen the will to live.'

In other words, prayer can have meaningful benefits, just like those derived from meditation, and also like those derived simply from being supportive and empathetic.

PRAYER AND MEDITATION

In reality, some kinds of prayer and some kinds of meditation amount to precisely the same thing. (If you'd like to be reminded about meditation techniques turn back to page 136.) Here are some key similarities:

- *inducing a feeling of calm*
- *realizing that there are things beyond immediate, everyday problems*
- *feeling a sense of connection*

- *gaining an insight into the nature of the universe*
- *seeking guidance*
- *becoming more positive.*

But if these benefits don't come from any direct intervention by a higher power, where do they come from? To some extent they come from *within you*, of course. The problem is that in our busy lives, particularly when we're under pressure, we just don't have the time to listen to our inner selves. We react, and often overreact, to outside events, losing our poise and our sense of being in control of our own destinies. Prayer and meditation restore our contact with our essential natures. Afterwards we feel more tranquil, more optimistic and have a clearer sense of direction. We have a better understanding of what it is we really want and what sort of people we truly are.

If, at the moment, you don't either pray or meditate, try it for a while and see what happens.

Insight
Some say that connection with our inner selves is not the whole story. Mystics believe that by going *inside* themselves, they're actually opening up a channel that reaches far *outside* themselves, to the essential nature of the universe.

How to be more spiritual if you don't believe in God

All truly religious people are spiritual but not all spiritual people are religious. In other words, even if you don't follow any religion and, what's more, even if you don't believe in God, you can still be a spiritual person.

That might sound paradoxical but it isn't at all. Religions are, to a large extent, codes of conduct and you're perfectly entitled to say you don't entirely agree with any of them. Of course, there are plenty of people who consider themselves to be, say, Christians or Jewish or Muslim without following all or, indeed, even most of the teachings. There's no reason you can't believe in the existence of God and have your own code of conduct.

What's more, even as a non-believer, you can still be spiritual and you can still have a code of conduct. Indeed, your own moral code might set a higher standard, as you see it, than some religions. Christians, for example, believe man has 'dominion' over animals. But there are many atheists who disagree and whose religion, as it were, is veganism. They believe it's morally wrong to cause suffering to animals.

As to the existence of God, well, Buddhism is universally recognized as a religion but its followers don't believe in one. And no one would say Buddhists weren't spiritual people.

But we're not concerned with religious arguments here. We're concerned with well-being and longevity and a set of beliefs that's helpful to both. As a non-believer, you can obviously still take part in regular, mutually supportive social activities other than going to church. And your spiritual feelings can be just as powerful as those of believers.

So what is this thing we call spirituality? Someone once said that it's impossible to define jazz but you know it when you hear it. It's very much the same with spirituality. And just as there are certain elements that can be identified in jazz, so there are, too, with spirituality.

PANTHEISM – SPIRITUAL ATHEISM

… leave the city – on a Sunday or a holiday – go into the deep countryside. Walk, walk until you no longer see the black smoke of the Petersburg chimneys behind you, and the limpid air of the horizon lies on you… Stop and reflect. How small you seem, how insignificant and helpless… And then – then, raise your eyes… A great tenderness will seize you… Later, you will venture further,

but for now return to the world. Go about your business while preserving, like the very apple of your eye, what you have brought back with you.

That's pantheism. Or is it? In fact, it's advice given by the 'mad Siberian monk' Rasputin to Prince Dzhevakov, as recalled by the prince in his memoirs, *Vospominaniya*. Rasputin did believe in God, of course. But with the phrases referring directly to God removed by me, his words do indeed sound very much like pantheism.

Pete Seeger used to define himself as an atheist. He just couldn't believe in an old man 'with a long white beard'. But now he has a new definition and says he's not an atheist any more. The folksinger believes God is *everything*. When he opens his eyes he's looking at God and when he hears something he's listening to God.

So, technically speaking, that makes Pete Seeger a pantheist. But definitions don't matter so much. What counts is that he's just as spiritual as any religious person.

Einstein had this to say: 'To sense that behind anything that can be experienced there is something that our mind cannot grasp and whose beauty and sublimity reaches us only indirectly and as a feeble reflection, this is religiousness. In this sense I am religious.' And Richard Dawkins, probably the UK's most famous atheist, agrees. In his book *The God Delusion*, he acknowledges that 'In this sense I too am religious.'

So there really isn't any need for religious people to fall out with one another over their slightly different beliefs, nor, indeed, for religious people to fall out with pantheists or atheists. Nevertheless, they do. But that's another issue.

If you feel concern for people you've never even met, if you give money to charity, if you live your life according to a high moral code even though it brings you no material reward, if you like to place your hands on the bark of a big old tree because you feel something when you do, if you're moved by a sunset, if you feel your life would be poorer if whales became extinct – even though you've never seen one – and if you take pleasure in the knowledge that life in all its many forms will continue long after you're dead, then all of that is spirituality.

Spirituality is more or less the opposite of materialism. That's not to say you can't be spiritual if you're rich or if you have a lot of possessions. But materialism is concerned with the tangible and spirituality is concerned with the intangible.

> ### Insight
> As we get older, we automatically tend to become less materialistic and more spiritual. When we're young, we see possessions as defining who we are. When we're older we realize it's our thoughts, feelings, actions and, sometimes, lack of action, that define who we are. It's what we have inside us and not what we surround ourselves with.

Developing spirituality

Highly spiritual people seem to exude something indefinable and yet instantly recognizable. They seem to attract others to them because we all want to know: What's the secret?

Well, what is? Is it something you're born with or is it something you can develop, just as you can develop other abilities? I believe you can cultivate your spirituality and, as a result, become a happier, more composed, tranquil person – and live longer.

Here are some exercises you might like to try.

DO SOMETHING GENEROUS IN SECRET

The nineteenth-century essayist Charles Lamb said the greatest pleasure he knew was to 'do a good action by stealth, and to have it found out by accident'. But I'm suggesting that each week you do something good or generous with no thought of accidental discovery, thanks or personal gain.

You might, for example, give some money anonymously to charity. Or maybe collect the rubbish along the side of a country lane. Or put in a good word for someone without that person knowing.

INCREASE YOUR CONNECTION WITH NATURE

Nature-worship is often associated with pantheism but, when you think about it, no one who believes in God should tolerate Creation being degraded. So do your bit to protect the environment. In addition, get out in the countryside whenever you can. Be sensual. Feel the grass, leaves, twigs and branches against your skin. Hug a tree. If you have a dog with you notice when he sniffs the air or the ground and you sniff too. Try to identify the scent. Let the breeze play on your skin. If there's a river, pond, lake or the sea, get into it. Swim naked, preferably. Feel the water. It's all about your connection with the rest of the universe.

NO CRITICISM

Try to spend a week without complaining about anything or criticizing anyone. It isn't easy. If you do manage it, try a further week.

CREATIVITY

Be creative in some way – it could be painting, music, writing, carpentry, dressmaking or whatever appeals to you. Many writers, artists and musicians believe their inspiration comes from somewhere outside of themselves. It's said that the musician and composer Arlo Guthrie believed there was a kind of stream of songs constantly flowing past him (and everyone else) and his gift was simply knowing the right moment to put out his hand and grab one.

Not all creative people would agree with that, especially given the years of study and training that can precede the making of a great work of art. But most would concede that there's something slightly mysterious in the process.

THE NIGHT SKY

One way of responding to the night sky is simply to stare at it. But sometimes it's the 'boring' statistics that underline what a truly astonishing universe we live in. So extraordinary, in fact, that the existence of God or Heaven or *something beyond* wouldn't be any more incredible than the facts we already know to be true.

See if you can spot Orion, the most brilliant group of stars. In winter you should easily see it rising due east, moving across the sky to the south of you, and setting due west. It's identified by three bright stars in a straight line, seemingly close together, and known as Orion's belt. A short way above the belt (and, in early winter, a little to the left) is an orangey star called Betelgeuse. Our own sun (a star) is the size of a *million* Earths. Now reflect that Betelgeuse is so much bigger again that if it were transposed with our sun we would actually be on the corona of Betelgeuse. Or to put it another way, Betelgeuse is so gigantic it could contain the entire orbit of the Earth around the sun, a diameter of something like 200 million miles.

Now just stare out into space generally and reflect that the furthest object so far recorded is 12 billion light years away, which means that, in effect, we're seeing it as it was 12 billion years ago. Not so long, relatively speaking, after the Big Bang. Now it may no longer even exist.

These kinds of things are scientific facts. But they're facts that do nothing to diminish the sense of awe and wonder at the universe. So get yourself a pair of binoculars and a star almanac and go outside on the next clear night. Say this to yourself: *Given what I'm looking at tonight, what isn't possible?*

Coping with death

It was the eighteenth-century American statesman Benjamin Franklin who made the famous observation: 'In this world nothing can be said to be certain, except death and taxes.'

As we get older we increasingly have to face up to the deaths of people we have known and loved and, ultimately, to our own end.

In Chapter 9 I wrote about the way love survives death. It's very important to remember that. If you have loved someone and been loved, that love will continue after death. You will carry it with you always. In the same way, you will always have your memories. The physical presence has gone, but so much remains.

Will you be reunited?

As I've suggested, go out on a clear night, look up at the stars and remember that phrase: *Given what I'm looking at tonight, what isn't possible?*

10 THINGS TO REMEMBER

1 *Most people have a need for a spiritual aspect to their lives.*

2 *Those who regularly attend a place of worship improve their chances of living longer.*

3 *Those who don't attend a place of worship but who nevertheless have religious or spiritual beliefs and feelings live slightly longer than those who have none.*

4 *Religious teaching generally promotes a positive and optimistic outlook that is conducive to longevity.*

5 *Religious belief generally makes it easier for people to cope with problems, avoid depression and face death.*

6 *But some religious teaching (such as a belief in Hell) is negative and is not conducive to longevity.*

7 *Prayers can bring benefits in the same way that meditation does.*

8 *Even if you don't follow any religion or believe in any god, you can still be a spiritual person and enhance your longevity.*

9 *Anyone can develop spirituality.*

10 *The universe is such a staggering place that it's hard to say anything is impossible, including life after death.*

HOW MUCH LONGER ARE YOU GOING TO LIVE NOW?

▶ *Do you regularly attend a place of worship together with others?*
▶ *Do you have religious or spiritual beliefs?*
▶ *Do you feel grateful for the good things in your life?*
▶ *Do you have religious or spiritual beliefs that help you cope with life's problems and make you feel optimistic?*
▶ *Do you pray and/or meditate?*
▶ *Do you sometimes do things to make the world a better place without any thought of thanks, reward or recognition?*
▶ *Do you feel connected to Nature?*
▶ *Do you feel your creativity has a mystical aspect?*
▶ *Do you have religious/spiritual beliefs that help you cope with the deaths of those close to you?*
▶ *Do you have religious/spiritual beliefs that help you cope with the idea of your own death?*

Score:

If you answered 'yes' to seven or more questions you're obviously a very religious and/or spiritual person and that's helpful for longevity.

If you answered 'yes' to between four and six questions you're quite spiritual but there are more religious/spiritual things you could easily do that, apart from their own worth, might improve your quality of life and your life expectancy.

If you answered 'yes' to three or fewer questions then you'd probably describe yourself as someone who is not very spiritual. It's not my role here to discuss the validity of various religious and spiritual beliefs, only to point out that holding such beliefs is generally positive for longevity. Read through the chapter again some time and think about the issues it raises. You may find that deep down you're more spiritual than you realized.

Taking it further

General

Live Longer, Feel Younger, Look Great, Diana Moran, Hamlyn, 2006

Maximum Energy, Ted Broer, Siloam Press, 2006

Turn Back Your Body Clock, Carina Norris, Headline, 2006

Food and supplements

Anatomy of an Illness, Norman Cousins, Norton, 2005

How to Live Longer and Feel Better, Linus Pauling, Freeman, 1986

Miracle Cures, Jean Carper, Harper Perennial, 1998

Stop Ageing Now, Jean Carper, Thorsons, 1997

Superyoung, Dr David Weeks and Jamie James, Hodder & Stoughton, 1998

The Food Pharmacy, Jean Carper, Pocket Books, 2000

www.crsociety.org
The website of The Calorie Restriction Society International. The society provides information on calorie restriction (CR) and promotes and carries out research.

www.walford.com
The website for the late gerontologist Dr Roy Walford, who pioneered the idea that restricting calorie intake could extend the human lifespan. Useful information and an Interactive Diet Planner providing analysis of some 3,000 foods into up to 28 macro and micro nutrients.

Exercise

Cycling for Health and Fitness, Bicycling Magazine, Rodale Press, 2000

Exercise, Health and Mental Health, Stuart J. H. Biddle, Routledge, 2005

Master the Art of Swimming, Steven Shaw, Collins & Brown, 2006

7-Week Cycling for Fitness, Chris Sidwells, DK Publishing, 2006

The Complete Guide to Walking for Health, Mark Fenton, The Lyons Press, 2001

The Runner's Handbook, Bob Glover, Penguin, 1996

Your brain

Brain Food, Lorraine Perretta, Hamlyn, 2004

How to Keep Your Brain Alive, Lawrence Katz, Manning Rubin, Workman Publishing, 1999

Saving Your Brain, Jeff Victoroff M. D., Bantam, 2003

Teach Yourself: Train Your Brain, Simon Wootton and Terry Horne, Hodder Education, 2010

The Mind Workout Book, Robert Allen, Collins & Brown, 2003

Relaxation

Awakening the Mind, Anna Wise, Tarcher Putnam, 2002

Teach Yourself: Relaxation Techniques, Alice Muir, Hodder Education, 2010

The Joy of Laziness, Michaela Axt-Gadermann and Peter Axt, Bloomsbury, 2005

Total Relaxation, Richard Latham, Meditainment, 2006

Happiness

Stumbling On Happiness, Daniel Gilbert, HarperPerennial, 2007

Teach Yourself: How to Be Happier, Paul Jenner, Hodder Education, 2010

The Art of Happiness, H H Dalai Lama and Howard Cutler, Coronet, 1999

The Science of Happiness, Stefan Klein, Marlowe & Company, 2002

www.depressionalliance.org
(Telephone: 0845 123 2320) Self-help groups all over the country for those suffering from depression, including the type known as involutional melancholia that can come on in middle age.

Prudence

Allen Carr's Easy Way to Stop Smoking, Allen Carr, Penguin, 2006

Arrive Alive: The Complete A–Z of Motorist's Safety, Graham Yuill, LDA, 1998

Mind Driving: New Skills for Staying Alive on the Road, Stephen Haley, DIA Publishing, 2006

No Big Deal: A Guide to Recovery from Addictions, John Coats, Sow's Ear Press, 2006

Say No to Cancer, Patrick Holford, Piatkus, 1999

Skin Cancer: Prevent and Survive, Tom Smith, Sheldon Press, 2006

Teach Yourself: Stop Smoking, Matthew Aldrich, Hodder Education, 2006

National Drugs Helpline – Free helpline 24/7: 0800 776 600

Drinkline – Free helpline: 0800 917 8282

www.alcoholics-anonymous.org.uk
Advice and support for those who have problems with alcohol.
Tel: 0845 769 7555

www.al-anonuk.org.uk
Advice and support for those affected by someone else's drinking.
Tel: 020 7403 0888

www.ash.org.uk
Information on the harmful effects of tobacco and how to give it up from Action on Smoking and Health (ASH).

www.preventcancer.com
Information about chemicals that can cause cancer.

Love and sex

Teach Yourself: Get Intimate with Tantric Sex, Paul Jenner, Hodder Education, 2010

Teach Yourself: Have Great Sex, Paul Jenner, Hodder Education, 2010

The Art of Loving, Erich Fromm, Thorsons, 1957

The Science of Love, Anthony Walsh, Ph.D, Prometheus Books, 1996

The Tao of Love, Jolan Chang, Wildwood House, 1977

Spirituality

Essential Spirituality, Roger Walsh, John Wiley & Sons, 2000

New Spirituality: An Introduction to Belief Beyond Religion, Gordon Lynch, I B Taurus & Co, 2007

World Religions, John Bowker, Dorling Kindersley, 2006

www.crusebereavementcare.org.uk
Telephone: 0844 477 9400. Support, information and advice for bereaved people.

www.federation-solo-clubs.co.uk
The National Federation of Solo Clubs for those who are lonely.

www.spiritualityhealth.com
A website that explores the soul/body connection.

The author

The author's website is at www.pauljenner.eu

Index